SATYRINAE part III

Tribe SATYRINI

Subtribes MELANARGIINA
and COENONYMPHINA

*Melanargia, Coenonympha,
Sinonympha, Triphysa*

Author: G C Bozano

GUIDE TO THE BUTTERFLIES OF THE PALEARCTIC REGION

Editor: G C Bozano

OMNES ARTES
Milano, October 2002

GUIDE TO THE BUTTERFLIES OF THE PALEARCTIC REGION
Satyrinae part III

ISBN 88-87989-03-6

author: Gian Cristoforo Bozano Viale Romagna, 76 - 20133 Milano (Italy) email: giancristoforo.bozano@eds.com
editor: Gian Cristoforo Bozano Viale Romagna, 76 - 20133 Milano (Italy) email: giancristoforo.bozano@eds.com
publisher: OMNES ARTES s.a.s.   Via Castel Morrone, 19 - 20134 Milano (Italy)

Foreword

The fourth volume of the GUIDE TO THE BUTTERFLIES OF THE PALEARCTIC REGION covers additional 56 species of Satyrinae belonging to the Subtribes Melanargiina and Coenonymphina.

Highly valuable sources of information for the preparation of this book have been the works on *Melanargia* by S. Wagener and the *Coenonympha* revision by D. Davenport.

Nevertheless the availability of new material from previously little known areas, together with today taxonomists' view that restricts the subspecific rank to taxa with well defined and constant diagnostic morphological features, have induced a number of changes in the previous taxonomic arrangements, including sinking into synonymy of some old taxa.

Although one of the main purposes of this book is to make clearer and to simplify the previous taxonomic arrangements, made heavy by too many confusing taxa, the introduction of a new subspecies of *Melanargia asiatica* has become necessary in order to identify a population showing clear and constant peculiar morphological features.

The book has mantained the same set up and structure of the first three volumes, as explained in the *How to use this guide* paragraph of the *Introduction*.

The author would like to express his thanks to Mr. P. Ackery, Mrs K. Goodger and Mr. J. Reynolds of the Entomology Department of the Natural History Museum, London, and to Mr. D. Stüning of the A. König Museum, Bonn for allowing unlimited access to their collections.

Grateful thanks go also to L. Arcelli, E. Balletto, S. Bossi, S. Churkin, C. Della Bruna, W. Eckweiler, A. Floriani, S. Sakai, V. Sbordoni, J. Verhulst, J. C. Weiss and M. Wiemers who contributed in different ways with suggestions, first hand information or pictures of little known taxa.

G. C. Bozano

Milano, October 2002

Introduction

The Palearctic Region

The Palearctic Region is a natural zoogeographic region that includes Europe, Africa north of the Sahara desert, most of the Middle-East, central Asia from the Himalayas to the Arctic Ocean and east to Korea and Japan.

The boundaries with the adjacent Afrotropical and Oriental regions are often not well defined and transition areas occur along the southern borders, where elements of the Afrotropical and Oriental fauna fly together with Palearctic species.

This guide will include:
- all the species occurring in the Palearctic region
- the species occurring in the transition areas, at an altitude above 2500-3000 metres
- the species that, even flying outside the Palearctic or the transition areas, belong to a Palearctic genus

In details the Palearctic region includes, from west to east:
- the islands of Azores, Madeira and Canaries
- all of Europe
- Africa roughly north of Tropic of Cancer, including all of Morocco, Algeria, Libya and Egypt, except the south-eastern Elba mountains
- the Arabian peninsula north of 26° N.
- Iran, except the south-eastern part
- Afghanistan
- northern and central Asia down to the Himalayas, including the transition area in northern Pakistan, northern India, Nepal and Bhutan where the border line follows the 3000 metres contour
- plateau of Tibet including its eastern slopes in N. Yunnan and W. Sichuan, but excluding the southern part of the Tsangpo valley
- China north of latitude 34 ° N, excluding the islands of Taiwan and Hainan.
- Japan, excluding the Ryukyu islands

The transition areas

The following transition areas have to be taken into consideration:
- the Arabian peninsula south of 26 ° N
- south-eastern Iran and the adjacent western Pakistan
- all the southern slopes of the Himalaya ridge
- western and central China, south of 34 ° N and north of a line starting at 26 ° N in the Yunnan plateau and going up to 32 ° N at the Yangtze outlet

No latitude or altitude criterion seems to objectively ascertain the inclusion or exclusion of a species from the Palearctic fauna.

The transition area in southern Arabian peninsula and in the Middle East, houses a mix of Palearctic, Afrotropical and Oriental species, often flying together, regardless of the altitude.

In the southern slopes of the Himalayas the 2500-3000 metres contour seems to set a reasonably good boundary between Palearctic and Oriental Lepidoptera fauna. Here the shift from one fauna to the other is quite sharp changing the altitude.

The situation is much more confusing in south-eastern Tibet and in south-western China, where, in large areas and in a big altitude range, species belonging to the Palearctic and to the Oriental fauna are flying together. The boundaries suggested in the literature are very discordant. Furthermore many genera found in these areas, *Neope* in the *Satyridae* and *Heliophorus* in the *Lycaenidae* are typical examples, have not an obvious Palearctic or Oriental identity, but they have to be assigned to an additional zoogeographic region, the Himalayan-Sino-Japanese one, which overlaps with both the Palearctic and the Oriental region. This subject has been developed with a lot of details by Palestrini, Simonis, Zunino (1985).

Taxonomic treatment

As stated by Corbet (1978), whether two forms are recognised as different species or are united in a single species, whether a species is included in genus A or in genus B, are subjective judgements made by the individual taxonomists.

This guide tries to show the current status of the classification of the Palearctic butterflies.

The taxa showing morphological discontinuities are here recognised as species. This is just a conventional criterion, and it is certainly too simplistic, but a critical review of the status of the many questionable butterfly taxa, with enzymes comparison and cross-breeding experiments, would involve a great deal of work, which is out of all proportion for the scope of this guide. As a result of the foregoing, most of the "strong" subspecies are treated here as good species, and the subspecific level is left to taxa showing the accentuation or the attenuation of one or more morphological characters somehow shown also by the nominal subspecies.

How to use this guide

For every Family, Subfamily, Tribe, Subtribe and Genus are given the essential **Diagnostic characters** and the **checklist** of the lower category taxa that are found and that are not found in the Palearctic region. These lists are arranged not in alphabetical, but in taxonomic order. The species lists include all existing subspecies. In the text the species are covered in the same order.

The type locality of each species is quoted just after the reference of the species' original description. The locality is shown both as in the original description and, in square brackets, with its current geographical name.

For the identification of the species, wherever possible, **Diagnostic characters** related to the wing pattern are given. If the wing pattern alone is not sufficient for an unambiguous identification, other anatomical characters are quoted.

Comments, if any, on the taxonomy of the species are given under the **Taxonomic note** heading.

As a general rule only the constant characters of a species are quoted. Identification characters that are not always present in that species are, wherever possible, not taken into consideration. For each species the variable characters and the existing subspecies, if any, are listed under the heading **Variation**.

For each species a distribution map is included under the **Range** heading.

A complete list of all the works from which any information has been taken for the compilation of this guide, is to be found in the **Bibliography**.

For easy reference, in every genus and species paragraph, works of particular interest, if any, are referred in the **Selected references** heading.

Illustrations

At least male upperside and underside are shown for each species. Significant variations, if any, are presented. Line drawings or pictures of the male genitalia of most species are also included.

Whenever possible the photographs have been taken by the authors from specimens belonging to private or public collections. In some cases the illustrations are reproduced from works of other authors, that are referred to under the picture.

For every illustration the origin of the specimen is quoted, as written in the specimen label.

Glossary and abbreviations

The wing venation and wing areas nomenclature adopted is shown in Fig. 1 and in Fig. 2.

The following abbreviations are used in the description of the diagnostic characters:

fw = forewing
hw = hindwing
ups = upperside
uns = underside
upf = upper forewing
unf = under forewing
uph = upper hindwing
unh = under hindwing

The following abbreviations, as suggested by Kudrna (1990), are used for the museums:

BMNH = British Museum Natural History, London
LNKD = Landesmuseum für Naturkunde, Karlsruhe
ZFMK = Zoologisches Musem "A. Koenig", Bonn
SZMN = Siberian Zoological Museum, Novosibirsk
ZIRP = Zoological Institute, Russian Academy of Sciences (St. Petersburg)
ZSMS = Zoologische Staatssammlung, München

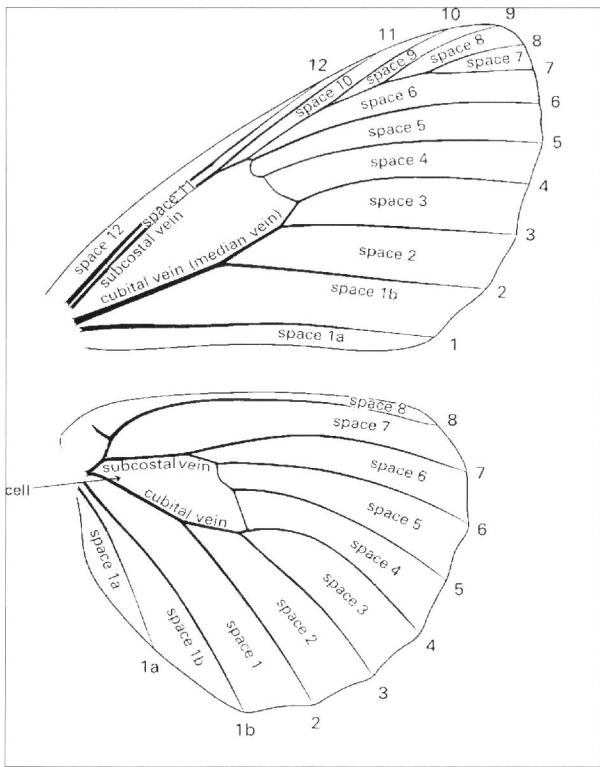

Fig. 1

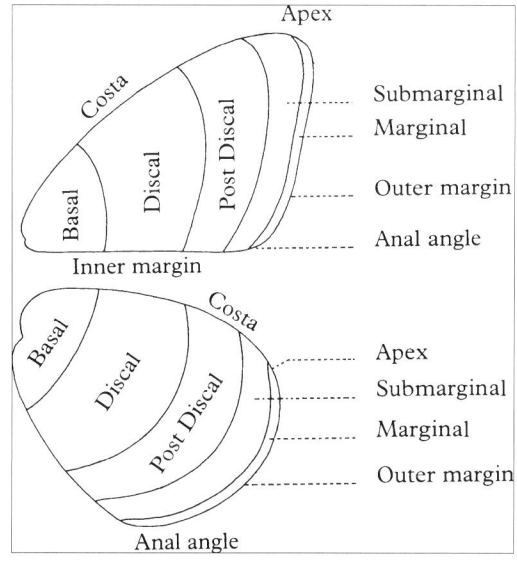

Fig. 2

Family **NYMPHALIDAE** Swainson, 1827

Starting from the second edition of Satyrinae Part II, an updated classification system of the butterflies has been considered in the series "Guide to te Butterflies of the Palearctic Region". In fact, at this time, we repute an array of improvements on the higher phylogeny of butterflies reached by cladistic evidence based on morphology, larval host plant relationships and molecular data as well, sufficiently robust to be adopted in the long run. This is not to say that the higher butterfly classification has reached a final assessment. Particularly the Nymphalid classification appears to be in continuous adjustment, starting from the seminal paper by Ehlirch (1958), followed by several relevant reviews including Ackery (1988), Harvey (1991), Martin and Pashley (1992), Ackery et al. (1999), Brower (2000).

From these contributions it appears that the best arrangement of the family Nymphalidae is that of Harvey (1991) with slight modifications introduced by Brower (2000), as reported in the website Butterfly Net International (http://www.ent.orst.edu/bnet/nymphali.htm), including the following subfamilies: Libytheinae, Heliconiinae, Nymphalinae, Limenitidinae, Charaxinae, Apaturinae, Morphinae (incl. Brassolinae), Satyrinae, Calinaginae and Danainae (incl. Tellervinae and Ithomiinae).

Subfamily **SATYRINAE** Boisduval, 1836

Satyrides Boisduval, 1836, Spec. Gen. Lep.: 166

The following definition of the family Satyridae was given by Miller (1968):

" No single key character will serve to separate the satyrids from all other nymphaloids, but a general definition of the Satyridae may be formulated as follows: a nymphaloid family having a larva with a bifid tail (fleshy anal projections from the eleventh abdominal segment) and feeding on monocotyledonous plants and generally having adults with the cells of the fore- and hindwings closed by tubular veins, forewing veins swollen at their bases and with more or less shaggy palpi. Only the habit of feeding on monocots and the bifid larval tail are universal in the Satyridae, and some morphids feed on monocotyledons. Many other nymphaloids (danaids, ithomiids, acraeines, etc.) have the cells of both wings closed by tubular veins, and the satyrid subfamily Ragadiinae is defined by *not* having the hindwing cell closed by tubular veins, often not closed at all. While many of the satyrids have shaggy palpi, many of the primitive ones have only very short hairs on the palpi. This part of the definition universally applies only to the temperate and arctic species. The forewing veins are usually, but not universally, swollen at their bases. The bases of the forewing veins of such satyrid genera as *Melanitis*, *Lethe*, *Oeneis* and *Melanargia* are less swollen than are those of such "true" nymphalid genera as *Mestra*, *Bolboneura* and *Callicore*."

Ehrlich (1958), who considered the Satyrinae a subfamily of the Nymphalidae, quoted the following anatomical characters to separate them: mesothoracic anepisternum is shown as a small, but distinct sclerite (also found in Charaxinae, Calinaginae and Morphinae); mesothoracic pre-episternum usually greatly reduced or, if not, separated from katepisternum by a very weak pre-episternal suture (Fig. 3).

The genitalic structures are often of great importance in specific and generic determination, but are not reliable for classification above the generic level (Miller, 1968).

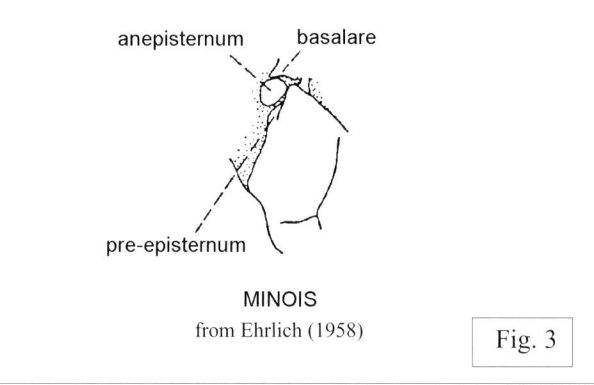

MINOIS
from Ehrlich (1958)

Fig. 3

Satyrinae represent by far the most diverse group of Nymphalid butterflies, approaching the 50% of the whole family. Ackery et al. (1999) calculate a total of 2400 species belonging to this subfamily which probably represent an underestimate, particularly in terms of biological species.

In the first two volumes of this guide the phenetic classification outlined by Miller (1968) was followed, treating this group as a family. Since then, several molecular phylogenetic advances on this group have been presented (Martin et al., 2000; Monteiro and Pierce, 2001; Nice and Shapiro, 2001; Torres et al., 2001; Sbordoni et al., 2002). These contributions help clarifying some aspects of the Satyrid classification, but also raise new problems. For instance, the study by Martin et al. (2000) based on the mitochondrial gene sequences of the large ribosomal subunit (16S rDNA), and the NADH dehydrogenase subunit 1 (ND1), highlights the systematic arrangement of the genus *Aphantophus*, formerly placed within Coenonymphina, in the Maniolina, and raises doubts on the monophyly of the genus *Erebia*. Also genus *Lyela*, previously included in the Coenonymphina, has to be moved since the comparison of molecular data shows that it is not related neither to the *Coenonympha* complex, nor to the *Callerebia* complex (V. Sbordoni in litteris).

As the Satyrids are now treated as a subfamily of the Nymphalidae, the taxonomic groups previously ranked as Subfamilies have to be downgraded to the rank of Tribes and the groups previously ranked as Tribes become now Subtribes. The *Melanargia* group and the *Coenonympha* group become therefore Subtribe Melanargiina and Subtribe Coenonymphina.

Based on this concerns we shall only consider a provisional arrangement of the Satyrinae in the following tribes: Haeterini, Melanitini, Elymniini, Eritini, Ragadiini and Satyrini.

TRIBES FOUND IN THE PALEARCTIC REGION
Elymniini Herrich-Schäffer, 1864
Melanitini Miller, 1968
Satyrini Boisduval, 1836

TRIBES NOT FOUND IN THE PALEARCTIC REGION
Eritini Miller, 1968
Haeterini Herrich-Schäffer, 1864
Ragadiini Herrich-Schäffer, 1864

Tribe **SATYRINI** Boisduval, 1836

Satyrides Boisduval, 1836, Histoire naturelle des Insectes. Spec. Gen. Lep.: 166

DIAGNOSTIC FEATURES
male foreleg greatly reduced;
number of subsegments in the female foretarsus generally fewer than five; in the few instances when five subsegments are found, then the whole tarsus is strongl club-like shaped;
forewing costal and median veins greatly swollen at their base (slightly swollen in the genus *Erebia*)

SUBTRIBES FOUND IN THE PALEARCTIC REGION
Melanargiina Wheeler, 1903
Satyrina Boisduval, 1836
Erebiina Tutt, 1896
Maniolina Hampson, 1918
Coenonymphina Miller, 1968
Ypthimina Miller, 1968

SUBTRIBES NOT FOUND IN THE PALEARCTIC REGION
Pronophilina Clark, 1947
Dirina Miller, 1968
Hypocystina Miller, 1968
Euptychiina Miller, 1968

Subtribe **MELANARGIINA** Wheeler, 1903

Melanargiinae Wheeler, 1903, The Butterflies of Switzerland and the Alps of Central Europe: 142
    = *Agapetinae* Verity, 1953, Le farfalle diurne d'Italia 5: 46

DIAGNOSTIC CHARACTERS
Eyes naked;
antennae about half the length of the forewing costa;
antennal club weakly developed;
male foreleg greatly reduced with a single unspined tarsal subsegment;
female foreleg reduced;
forewing cell square and about half the length of the forewing costa;
forewing only the subcostal vein inflated at the base;
wing pattern quite distinctive: ground colour white marbled with black and with well developed submarginal ocelli

CHECKLIST OF THE GENERA
Melanargia Meigen, 1829

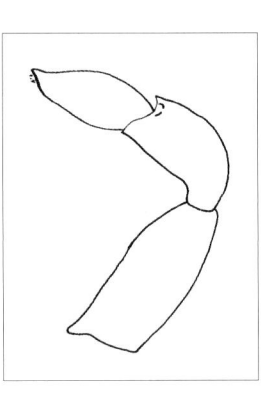
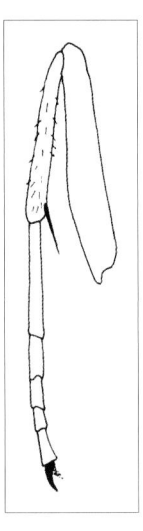
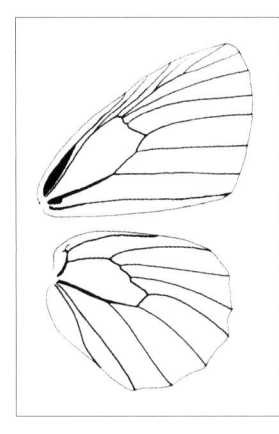

Melanargia galathea
♂ foreleg
from Miller (1968)

Melanargia galathea
midleg
from Miller (1968)

Melanargia galathea
♂ venation
from Miller (1968)

genus **MELANARGIA** Meigen, 1829

Melanargia Meigen, 1829, Syst. Beschr. Europ. Schmett. 1: 97
Type species: *Papilio galathea* Linnaeus, 1758 (by selection by Kirby 1894, in Allen's Nat. Libr., Lepid. 1: 240)
   = *Agapetes* Billberg, 1820, Enum. Insect. Mus. G. J.: 78
   = *Arge* Hübner, 1819, Samml. Exot. Schmett.: 60
   = *Argeformia* Verity, 1953, Le farfalle diurne d'Italia 5: 47
   = *Epimede* Houlbert, 1922, Etud. Lep. comp. 19: 132
   = *Halimede* Oberthür and Houlbert, 1922, Etud. Lep. comp. 19: 192
   = *Lachesis* Oberthür and Houlbert, 1922, Etud. Lep. comp. 19: 192
   = *Ledargia* Houlbert, 1922, Etud. Lep. comp. 19: 157
   = *Parce* Oberthür and Houlbert, 1922, Etud. Lep. comp. 19: 193

DIAGNOSTIC FEATURES
See under Tribe *Melanargiini*

RANGE
Found only in the Palearctic region

SELECTED REFERENCES
Mensi et al. (1990), Miller (1968)

CHECKLIST OF THE SPECIES
galathea galathea (Linnaeus, 1758)
   galathea satnia Fruhstorfer, 1917
   galathea magdalenae Reichl, 1975
   galathea syracusana Zeller, 1847
lucasi (Rambur, 1858)
lachesis (Hübner, 1790)
evartiane Wagener, 1976
teneates teneates (Ménétriés, 1832)
   teneates meda (Grum-Grshimailo, 1895)
titea titea (Klug, 1832)
   titea titania Calberla, 1891
   titea standfussi Wagener, 1983
   titea wiskotti Rober, 1896
larissa larissa (Geyer, 1828)
   larissa taurica (Rober, 1896)
   larissa massageta (Staudinger, 1901)
grumi Standfuss, 1892
hylata hylata (Ménétriés, 1832)
   hylata iranica Seitz, 1907
syriaca syriaca (Oberthür, 1894)
   syriaca kocaki Wagener, 1893
   syriaca karabagi (Koçak, 1976)
occitanica occitanica (Esper, 1793)
   occitanica pelagia (Oberthür, 1911)
   occitanica pherusa (Boisduval, 1832)
ines (Hoffmannsegg, 1804)
arge (Sulzer, 1776)

russiae russiae (Esper, 1793)
   russiae cleanthe (Boisduval, 1833)
   russiae japygia (Cyrillo, 1787)
   russiae eberti Wagener, 1975
parce Staudinger, 1882
leda leda Leech, 1891
   leda yunnana (Oberthür, 1891)
   leda melli Wagener, 1961
halimede halimede (Ménétriés, 1858)
   halimede halimedina Bryk, 1947
   halimede coreana Okamoto, 1926
   halimede gratiani Wagener, 1961
meridionalis (Felder C.&R., 1862)
montana (Leech, 1890)
lugens lugens (Honrath, 1888)
   lugens ahyoui Wagener, 1961
   lugens hengshanensis Wagener, 1961
   lugens hoenei Wagener, 1961
epimede epimede (Staudinger, 1887)
   epimede pseudolugens (Forster, 1942)
ganymedes (Heyne, 1895)
asiatica asiatica Oberthür & Houlbert, 1922
   asiatica dejeani Wagener, 1961
   asiatica elisa Wagener, 1961
   asiatica wageneri **ssp. nov.**

MELANARGIA GALATHEA (Linnaeus, 1758)

♂ ups — ssp *galathea* — Val Gesso, Maritim Alps, Italy
♂ ups — ssp *galathea* — Cimon del Grappa, Vicenza, Italy
♀ ups — ssp *galathea* — Cogne, Aosta Valley, Italy

♂ uns
♂ uns
♀ uns

♀ uns — f. *leucomelas* — Como, Italy

♂ ups — ssp *satnia* — Kastania, Pindus, Greece
♀ ups — ssp *satnia* — Kastania, Pindus, Greece

♂ uns
♀ uns

♂ ups — ssp *magdalenae* — Barcis, Friuli, Italy
♂ uns
♀ ups — ssp *magdalenae* — Barcis, Friuli, Italy
♀ uns

Papilio galathea Linnaeus, 1758, Syst. Nat. (ed. 10) 1: 474
Type locality: australioris Europa [Germany]
  – *akis* Fruhstorfer, 1910, Ent. Zeit. 23: 241
  – *apicalis* Turati, 1919, Atti Soc. ital. Sci. nat. 58: 148
  – *arogna* Fruhstorfer, 1920, Arch. Naturgesch. 86: 109
  – *calabra* Verity, 1913, Boll. Soc. ent. Ital. 45: 215
  – *doris* Fruhstorfer, 1910, Ent. Zeit. 23: 240
  – *florentina* Verity, 1919, Ent. Rec. 31: 125
  – *galatea* Herrich-Schäffer, 1844, Schmett. Eur. 1: 53
  – *galataea* Ochsenheimer, 1807, Schmett. Eur. I, 1: 242
  – *galinthias* Fruhstorfer, 1920, Arch. Naturgesch. 82: 21
  – *nereus* Fruhstorfer, 1910, Ent. Zeit. 23: 240
  – *panormitana* Verity, 1919, Ent. Rec. 31: 125
  – *pedemonti* Verity, 1927, Ent. Rec. 39: 125
  – *procida* Herbst, 1796, Natur. Ins. 8: 22
  – *serena* Verity, 1912, Boll. Soc. ent. Ital. 44: 205
Extensive lists of synonyms and individual forms can be found in Gaede (1931), Gaede (1939) and in Verity (1953)

DIAGNOSTIC CHARACTERS
upf cell without transverse black bar;
upf basal and distal areas of cell black (this character is not constant: the basal area is white in specimens with reduced black markings and in ssp *syracusana)*;
hw cell largely encircled with grey-black, except in space 5 where usually the black suffusion becomes very thin (a)

VARIATION
very variable:
ups black suffusion is variable and the prevalence of dark or light forms is scattered through the whole range, without the correlation between dark forms in humid areas and dry forms in arid areas that is found in most butterflies species; light forms are usual in S. England, N. W. France, N. Spain, but are found also in the Alps and in Sicily; dark forms are usual in S. E. France, S. Italy and N. E. Italy.
In the Balkans, Greece, Turkey and Caucasus the black suffusion is well pronounced and more constant, therefore a subspecific status seems to be justified for those populations (ssp *satnia).*
In a restricted area in N. E. Italy the extremely darkened form *magdalenae* Reichl, 1975 is almost constant therefore the status of subspecies seems well deserved.
Ground colour yellow instead of white: f. *flava* Fritsch, 1911, Int. ent. Zeit. 5: 220;
unh unmarked, uniformly white: f. *leucomelas* Esper, 1782, Schmett. 1: 2;
unh ocelli obsolete or absent: f. *galene* Ochsenheimer, 1807, Schmett. 1: 236;

ssp *satnia* Fruhstorfer, 1917
Melanargia galathea satnia Fruhstorfer, 1917, Soc. ent. 32: 5
Type locality: Maglis [Kazanluk], Bulgaria
  – *donsa* Fruhstorfer, 1920, Arch. Naturgesch. 82: 20
  – *syntelia* Fruhstorfer, 1916, Soc. ent. 31: 34
  – *tenebrosa* Fruhstorfer, 1917, Soc. ent. 32: 6
  – *turcica* Boisduval, 1840, Genera et Index Metodicus: 25
ups heavily suffused with black;
upf white area in the cell smaller than in nominal *galathea* (b)

ssp *magdalenae* Reichl, 1975
Melanargia galathea magdalenae Reichl, 1975, Zeitschrift ArbGem. ost. Ent. 26: 33
Type locality: Barcis, Friuli [N.E.Italy]
  – *tramontina* Reichl, 1975, Zeitschrift ArbGem. ost. Ent. 26: 34
upf almost completely black

♂ ups

♂ ups

♂ uns

♂ uns

ssp *magdalenae*
Bosplans, Friuli, Italy

ssp *syracusana*
Ficuzza, Palermo, Sicily

♂ genitalia

ssp *galathea*
C. France
from Higgins (1975)

valva
ssp *galathea*
C. France
from Higgins (1975)

ssp *syracusana* Zeller, 1847
Melanargia galathea syracusana Zeller, 1847, Isis von Oken: 143
Type locality: Siracusa, Sicily
    – *sicula* Stauder, 1928, Lep. Rdsch. Wien 2: 108
upf basal area of cell white or little suffused with black (c) (not constant)

TAXONOMIC NOTE
In spite of many investigations, the relationship between taxa *galathea*, *lachesis* and *lucasi* seems till not at all clear; some authors rank them as three good species, while others treat *lachesis* and *lucasi* as subspecies of *galathea*, or *lachesis* as a good species and *lucasi* as subspecies of *galathea*; male genitalia, that are similar and variable, provide limited help.
The arrangement adopted here follows the results obtained by Wagener (1984) who, on the basis of the morphology of the eggs, ranked *lachesis* as a good species. More recent studies on the populations found in the contact area between *galathea* and *lachesis* [Mazel (1986) and Mensi et al. (1990)] have given further support to this position

RANGE
ssp *galathea*: Europe from N. Spain to Lithuania, S. Urals and Crimea
ssp *magdalenae*: N. E. Italy
ssp *satnia*: S. E. Europe from Slovenia to Greece, Asia Minor and Transcaucasus
ssp *syracusana*: Sicily

SELECTED REFERENCES
Descimon & Renon (1975), Hesselbarth et al. (1995), Higgins (1975), Merit (1996), Verity (1953)

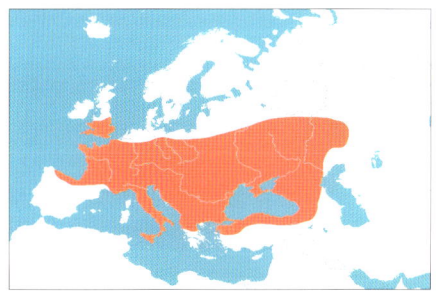

MELANARGIA LUCASI (Rambur, 1858)

a

b

♂ ups

♀ ups

c

b

♂ uns

♀ uns

Tizi-n-Tichka, Morocco

Ifrane, Middle Atlas, Morocco

♂ genitalia: valva
Algeria, from Higgins (1975)

Arge lucasi Rambur, 1858, Catal. Lep. Andal.: 20
Type locality: Bougie [Bejaia, Algeria]
    – *mauritanica* Oberthür, 1876, Etud. ent. 1: 26
    – *meadewaldoi* Rotschild, 1917, Novit. Zool. 24: 210

DIAGNOSTIC CHARACTERS
upf cell without transverse black bar;
upf basal area of cell white or little suffused with black (a);
hw both sides cell encircled with black usually also in space 5 (b);
uph veins firmly black-lined;
unf cell closed distally by a black bar (c)

VARIATION
ups black markings vary individually, but generally the variation is clinal from forms with heavy black markings found in Morocco, to forms with large white areas in Tunisia

TAXONOMIC NOTE
See under *M. galathea*

RANGE
N. Africa

SELECTED REFERENCES
Tennent (1996)

MELANARGIA LACHESIS (Hübner, 1790)

σ ups   ♀ ups

σ genitalia: valva

Bronchales, Spain, from Higgins (1975)

σ uns   ♀ uns

Gerona, Spain   Mont Louis, Pyrenees Orient., France

Papilio lachesis Hübner, 1790, Beitr. Schmett. Vol. 2: 70
Type locality: Languedoc (France)
 – *alta* Oberthür, 1909, Lepid. Comp. 3: 351
 – *barcinonaria* de Sagarra, 1924, Butll. Inst. catal.
 Hist. nat. 4: 198
 – *canigulensis* Berce, 1867, Lep. Fr. 1: 185
 – *catalana* de Sagarra, 1926, Butll. Inst. catal. Hist.
 nat. 26: 134
 – *escorialensis* Oberthür, 1909, Lepid. Comp. 3: 354
 – *lundbladi* Bryk, 1940, Ark. Zool. 32A: 10
 – *nemausiaca* Esper, 1790, Schmett. 1: 96
 – *olaria* Ribbe, 1909, Dt. ent. Z. Iris 23: 151
 – *rutae* Bryk, 1940, Ark. Zool. 32A: 11
 An extensive list of synonyms and individual forms
 can be found in Gaede (1931)

DIAGNOSTIC CHARACTERS
upf cell without transverse black bar;
upf basal area of cell white or little suffused with
black (a);
upf black rectangular spot in space 3 adjacent to cell (b);
uph spaces 2, 3, 4 and 5 around the cell white or light
grey (c) (black, except in space 5, in *M. galathea*)

VARIATION
ups extension of dark suffusion variable;
unh unmarked, uniformly white: f. *cataleuca* Staudinger,
1871, Catal. Lep. Pal. Fauna ed. 2: 22

TAXONOMIC NOTE
See under *M. galathea*

RANGE
Spain, Portugal, S. E. France

SELECTED REFERENCES
Jutzeler (1994), Mazel (1986), Mensi et al. (1990),
Wagener (1984b)

MELANARGIA EVARTIANE Wagener, 1976

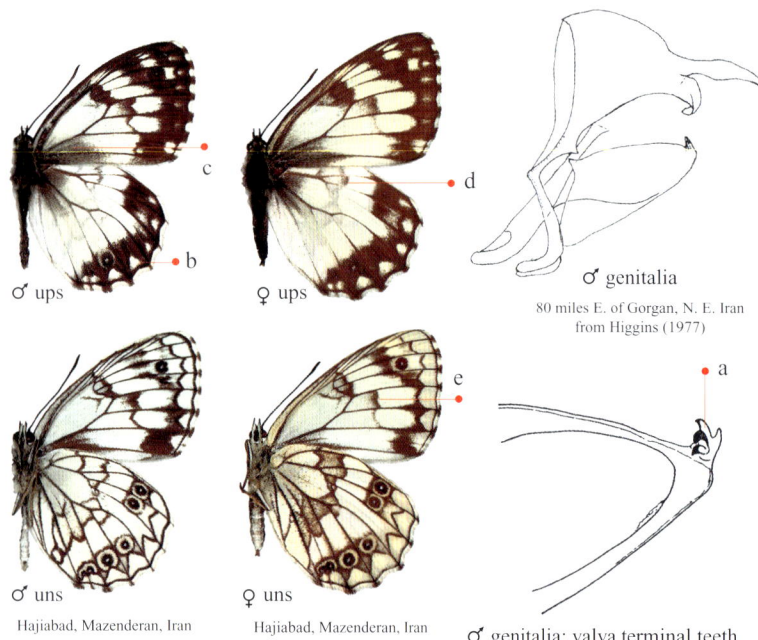

σ ups   ♀ ups

σ genitalia

80 miles E. of Gorgan, N. E. Iran
from Higgins (1977)

σ uns   ♀ uns

Hajiabad, Mazenderan, Iran   Hajiabad, Mazenderan, Iran

σ genitalia: valva terminal teeth
from Wagener (1976)

Melanargia evartiane Wagener, 1976, J. Ent. Soc. Iran
3: 75
Type locality: Gorgan valley, 50 km E. of Minudasht,
N. Iran
 – *origo* Higgins, 1977, Ent. Rec. 89: 189

DIAGNOSTIC CHARACTERS
male genitalia: valva with 4 or 5 terminal teeth (a) (over
ten teeth in all similar species;
ups veins strongly outlined with black;
ups marginal white spots well pronounced (b);
upf cell without transverse black bar;
upf basal dark suffusion in space 1 less distally extended
than in *M. teneates* (c);
uph black linear markings between cell and costa in
spaces 6 and 7 (d) (black spot in *M. teneates*);
unf black linear or triangular spot in space 3 not reaching
the cell (e) (spot rectangular and reaching the cell in
M. teneates)

RANGE
N. E. Iran

SELECTED REFERENCES
Wagener (1980b)

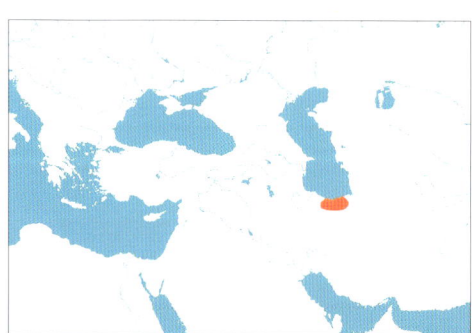

MELANARGIA TENEATES (Ménétriés, 1832)

ssp *teneates*
Talysch, Azerbaijan

ssp *teneates*
Gillan prov., N. Iran

intermediate between ssp
teneates and ssp *meda*
Rudbar, N. Iran (by W. Eckweiler)

ssp *meda*
Sardob Rud, Elburs, Iran

ssp *meda*
Gillan prov., Iran

ssp *meda*
Kendevan, Elburs, Iran

Satyrus teneates Mènétriés, 1832, Lepidoptera. In: Cat. rais. zool. Caucase: 252
Type locality: Zouvant, Talyche [Talysh, S. Azerbaijan]

DIAGNOSTIC CHARACTERS
male genitalia: valva with 10 to 18 terminal teeth (a);
ups veins not strongly outlined with black;
upf cell without transverse black bar;
upf basal area of cell white or little suffused with black;
upf basal dark suffusion in space 1 more distally extended than in *M. evartiane* (b);
uph large black spot between cell and costa in spaces 6 and 7 (c) (only a line in *M. evartiane*)

VARIATION
ssp *meda* Grum-Grshimailo, 1895 **stat. nov.**
Melanargia meda Grum-Grshimailo, 1895, Horae Soc. ent. ross. 29: 291
Type locality: Persia, in declivitate meridionali montium Elburs [Damavend, N. Iran]
– *elbursica* De Lesse, 1971, Alexanor 7: 156
black markings more developed than in nominal *teneates*:
fw black postdiscal spot in space 3 usually large and rectangular (d);
upf black spot at cell end larger than in nominal *teneates* (e);
upf space 2 crossed by a dark line (f) (absent in nominal *teneates* and in *M. evartiane*);
specimens with heavy dark suffusion resemble *M. galathea*, but in hw both sides the cell is completely surrounded by dark grey, as in *M. lucasi* (g)

TAXONOMIC NOTE
The shape of male genitalia, the distribution ranges and the presence of populations with intermediate characters (Eckweiler pers. comm.), suggest taxa *teneates* and *meda* to be conspecific; it seems even possible that light nominal *teneates* and dark forms of *meda* are the two ends of a cline, in which case *meda* would have to be downgraded to synonym of *teneates*

RANGE
ssp *teneates*: S. E. Azerbajan, N. W. Iran
ssp *meda*: N. Iran

SELECTED REFERENCES
Wagener (1976)

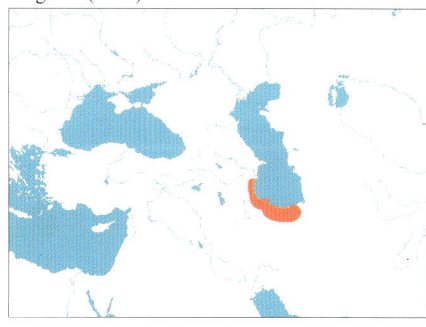

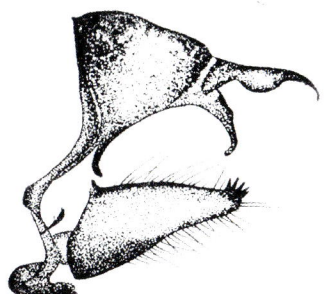

ssp *teneates*
♂ genitalia
from Nekrutenko (1990)

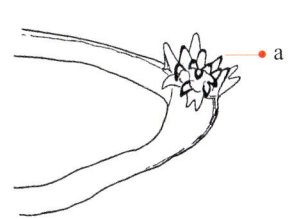

ssp *meda*
♂ genitalia: valva terminal teeth
Sardab valley, Elburs, Iran
from Wagener (1976)

MELANARGIA TITEA (Klug, 1832)

ぷ ups   ♀ ups   ♂ ups   ♀ ups

♂ uns   ♀ uns   ♂ uns   ♀ uns

ssp *titea*
Kesrouane, Lebanon

ssp *titea*
Chouf, Lebanon

ssp *titania*
Jarash, Jordan

ssp *titania*
Ajlun, Jordan

♂ ups   ♀ ups   ♂ ups   ♀ ups

♂ uns   ♀ uns   ♂ uns   ♀ uns

ssp *standfussi*
Gaziantep, Turkey

ssp *standfussi*
Gaziantep, Turkey

ssp *wiskotti*
Mersin, Turkey

ssp *wiskotti*
Silifke, Turkey

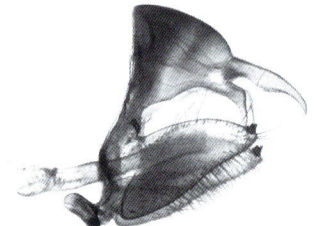

ssp *titea*
♂ genitalia
Beit ed Din, Lebanon

Hipparchia titea Klug, 1832, Insecta. In Hemprich & Ehrenberg Symb. Phys. pl. 29 fig. 15-18
Type locality: Habitat in Syria [Beirut, Lebanon]
    – *arceti* Lefebvre, 1832, Annls. Soc. ent. Fr. 1: 89
    – *darceti* Duponchel, 1832, in Godart: Histoire Naturelle des Lépidoptères ou Papillons de France 1: 174

DIAGNOSTIC CHARACTERS
upf basal area of cell white or little suffused with black (a);
upf postdiscal black spot in space 3 large and rectangular (b) (showing only black edges in subspecies *standfussi* and *wiskotti*)

VARIATION
ssp *titania* Calberla, 1891
Melanargia titea titania Calberla, 1891, Dt. ent. Z. Iris 4: 41
Type locality: Hauran [Jabal ad Duruz, Syria]
    – *palestinensis* Staudinger, 1901, in Staudinger & Rebel Catal. Lep. Pal. Fauna: 42
ups with reduced black markings

ssp *standfussi* Wagener, 1983
Melanargia titea standfussi Wagener, 1983, Nota Lepid 6: 185
Type locality: Urfa, Gaziantep, S. E. Turkey
ups black markings usually less developed than in ssp *titania*;
ups wing base little suffused with black;
upf black spot in the distal area of the cell reduced to two black lines (c)

ssp *wiskotti* Röber, 1896
Melanargia titea wiskotti Röber, 1896, Ent. Nachr. Berlin 22: 83
Type locality: Dorak [Mersin, S. Turkey]
larger than the other subspecies;
ups wing base little suffused with black;
ups submarginal black band well developed (d);
upf black spot in the distal area of the cell reduced to two black lines (c)

TAXONOMIC NOTE
The validity of the above subspecies is questionable because in many localities *M. titea* shows a graduated series of forms going to one subspecies to the other

RANGE
ssp *titea*: Lebanon
ssp *titania*: N. Israel, N. Jordan, W. Syria, S. E. Turkey (Antakya prov.)
ssp *standfussi*: S. E. Turkey (Gaziantep prov.), N. Syria
ssp *wiskotti*: S. Turkey (Mersin and Adana prov.)

SELECTED REFERENCES
Hesselbarth et al. (1995), Larsen (1974), Wagener (1983a)

MELANARGIA LARISSA (Geyer, 1828)

ssp *larissa*
Prilep, Macedonia

ssp *larissa*
Yugoslavian coast

form *herta*
Gulin, Sibenik, Yugoslavia

form *herta*
Yugoslavian coast

ssp *larissa* from "*lesbina*" range
Gallipoli, European Turkey

ssp *larissa* from "*noacki*" range
Palandoken, Erzurum, Turkey

ssp *larissa* from "*noacki*" range
Bala, Ankara, Turkey

ssp *larissa* from "*astanda*" range
Ardahan, Posof, Turkey

ssp *taurica*
Beysehir, Toros Dag., Konia, Turkey

ssp *taurica*
Geris, Toros Dag., Antalya, Turkey

Papilio larissa Geyer, 1828, in Hübner, Sammlg. eur. Schmett. pl. 182 fig. 896-899
Type locality: Cherso [Cres Island, Croatia]
   – *astanda* Boisduval, 1848 **syn. nov**.
   Arge astanda Boisduval, 1848, Bull. Soc. ent. Fr. (2) 6: 29
   – *herta* Hübner, 1828, Sammlg. eur. Schmett. pl. 183 fig. 900-903
   – *hertina* Staudinger, 1901, in Staudinger & Rebel, Catal. Lep. Pal. Fauna: 42
   – *lesbina* Wagener, 1976 **syn. nov**.
   Melanargia larissa lesbina Wagener, 1976, Nachr. Bl. bayer. Ent. 25: 40
   – *lydia* Fruhstorfer, 1916, Soc. ent. 32: 33
   – *noacki* Wagener, 1983 **syn. nov**.
   Melanargia larissa noacki Wagener, 1983, Atalanta 14: 286
   taxa *astanda*, *lesbina* and *noacki* do not show any reliable diagnostic character and specimens from their supposed ranges vary within the usual area of variation of nominal *larissa*.
   An extensive list of synonyms and individual forms can be found in Gaede (1931)

DIAGNOSTIC CHARACTERS
ups basal and discal areas heavily suffused with dark grey;
upf cell basal area suffused with grey (a);
upf fine dark line crossing the cell, closer to the cell distal end than in *M .russiae* (b);
unh black markings well defined, except in ssp *massageta* (markings are yellow-brown, soft or obsolete in *M. hylata*)

VARIATION
size and extension of the black markings are very variable; f. *herta*, common in some areas in the Balkans, shows a reduced discal dark suffusion.

ssp *taurica* Röber, 1896
Melanargia astanda taurica Röber, 1896, Ent. Nachr. 22: 83
Type locality: Dorak und Gülen [W. Taurus, Turkey]
   – *wageneri* Koçak, 1977, Atalanta 8: 129
ups black suffusion prominent and clearly separated from the white areas

ssp *massageta* Staudinger, 1901
Melanargia grumi massageta Staudinger, 1901, in Staudinger & Rebel Catal. Lep. Pal. Fauna: 42
Type locality: Malatia (Kurd. oc.) [Malatya, Turkey]
ups marginal areas with white spots larger than in other subspecies;
unf submarginal marking at wing apex light brown or obsolete (black in other subspecies);
unh markings yellow-brown or obsolete, as in *M. hylata* (black in other subspecies);
transition forms between ssp *massageta* and nominal *larissa* are common in a large area around the range of typical *massageta* (see pictures in the following page)

13

♂ ups ♀ ups

♂ uns ♀ uns

ssp *massageta* ssp *massageta*

Sivas, Turkey Sivas, Turkey

♂ genitalia
Ibarska klisura
from Jaksic (1998)

TAXONOMIC NOTE
The distinction between taxa *larissa*, *grumi*, *hylata* and *syriaca* is often extremely difficult and their taxonomic status has yet to be fully understood.
Male genitalia are very variable and do not give valuable help.
The study of eggs morphology by Wagener (1984a) has provided elements to support their status of good species.

RANGE
ssp *larissa*: Balkans, Greece, Bulgaria, Turkey, Caucasus, N. Iraq
ssp *taurica*: W. Taurus Mts. in S. W. Turkey
ssp *massageta*: S. E. Turkey

SELECTED REFERENCES
Ercolino (1997), Hesselbarth et al. (1995), Wagener (1983b)

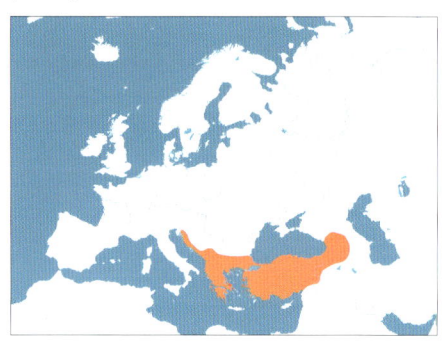

MELANARGIA GRUMI Standfuss, 1892

a •

b •

♂ ups ♂ ups ♀ ups

♂ uns ♂ uns ♀ uns

Mesopotamia, Turkey Mesopotamia, Turkey Mesopotamia, Turkey

♂ genitalia
50 km east of Gulnar,
Turkey

Melanargia grumi Standfuss, 1892, in Romanoff 6: 661
Type locality: Mardin, Kurdistan [S. E. Turkey]

DIAGNOSTIC CHARACTERS
ups ground colour yellowish, black markings strongly reduced (both characters not constant);
upf cell basal area with grey suffusion light or obsolete;
upf thin black line crossing the cell not as close to cell end as in *M. titea* (a);
uph dark basal suffusion absent or vestigial (b)

VARIATION
ups ground colour pure white and black markings well developed in some specimens;
unh black markings sometimes obsolete as in *M. larissa massageta*

TAXONOMIC NOTE
Treated by many authors as a subspecies of *M. larissa*; the status of good species has been confirmed by Wagener (1984a) on the basis of egg morphology

RANGE
S. E. Turkey

SELECTED REFERENCES
Hesselbarth et al. (1995)

MELANARGIA HYLATA (Ménétriés, 1832)

♂ ups

♂ ups

♀ ups

ssp *hylata*

Zuvand, Talysch, Azerbaijan

♂ uns

ssp *hylata*

Karaj Mt., Tehran, Iran

♂ uns

ssp *hylata*

Kandovan, Mazandaran, Iran

♀ uns

♀ ups

♂ ups

♀ ups

♀ uns

ssp *hylata*

Yuksekova, Hakkari, Turkey

♂ uns

ssp *iranica*

Dasht-e-Arjan, Fars, Iran

♀ uns

ssp *iranica*

Dasht-e-Arjan, Fars, Iran

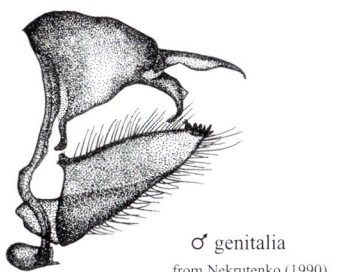

♂ genitalia

from Nekrutenko (1990)

Satyrus hylata Ménétriés, 1832, Catal. Rais.: 251
Type locality: Khanat de Talyche [Talyshskiye Gory, Azerbaijan and N. Iran]

DIAGNOSTIC CHARACTERS
wing fringes very long;
ups basal area heavily suffused with dark grey;
upf cell basal area suffused with grey (a);
upf dark line crossing the cell closer to the cell distal end than in *M .russiae* (b);
upf median black spot in space 3 large and rectangular (c);
unf submarginal markings at wing apex little developed or obsolete;
uph cell encircled with black (d);
unh black markings little developed or obsolete

VARIATION
size variable;
ups extension of dark markings variable;
unh dark markings completely absent in some specimens

ssp *iranica* Seitz, 1907
Melanargia hylata iranica Seitz, 1907, Grosschmett. d. Erde 1: 116
Type locality: Shiraz [Iran]
usually larger than nominal *hylata*;
uph median white band very large, with veins little or not at all lined with black (e);
uns black marginal line separating the white marginal area from the white fringes, obsolete or absent (f)

TAXONOMIC NOTE
See under *Melanargia larissa*

RANGE
ssp *hylata*: Azerbaijan, E. Turkey, N. Iran, N. Iraq
ssp *iranica*: C. Iran (Fars region)

SELECTED REFERENCES
Hesselbarth et al. (1995)

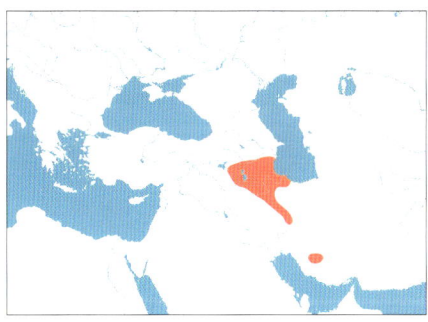

15

MELANARGIA SYRIACA (Oberthür, 1894)

♂ ups   ♀ ups

♂ uns   ♀ uns

ssp *syriaca*
Nurdagi Gec., Adana, Turkey

ssp *syriaca*
Shar-Deresy, N. Syria

♂ genitalia
ssp *syriaca*
Nurdagi Gec., Adana,
Turkey

♂ ups   ♂ ups   ♂ ups   ♀ ups

♂ uns   ♂ uns   ♂ uns   ♀ uns

ssp *kocaki*
Kavusshap Dag., Van, Turkey

ssp *kocaki*
Tunceli, Pertek, Turkey
from Hesselbarth et al. (1995)

ssp *karabagi*
Otluca, Hakkari, Turkey

ssp *karabagi*
Otluca, Hakkari, Turkey

Arge galathea syriaca Oberthür, 1894, Etud. ent. 19: 18
Type locality: Akbès (Syrie) [Amanos Mts., Antakya, S. Turkey]
   – *gnophos* Oberthür, 1894, Etud. ent. 19: 19

DIAGNOSTIC CHARACTERS
upf cell completely covered by brown-black shading

VARIATION
size variable;
ups and uns extension of dark markings variable;
the melanic form has been described as *gnophos*

ssp *kocaki* Wagener, 1983
Melanargia syriaca kocaki Wagener, 1983, Atalanta 14: 257
Type locality: Murat river valley, E. Anatolia [E. Turkey]
upf white submarginal spots usually present (a) (usually absent in nominal *syriaca*);
uns ground colour creamy (usually pure white in nominal *syriaca*);
unf without basal dark suffusion in space 1b (b)

ssp *karabagi* Koçak, 1976
Melanargia larissa karabagi Koçak, 1976, Atalanta 7: 40
Type locality: Hakkari [E. Turkey]
ups almost completely covered by dark brown scales;
uph white median band less pronounced than in nominal *syriaca* (c);
uns ground colour creamy (usually pure white in nominal *syriaca*)

TAXONOMIC NOTE
See under Melanargia larissa.
The population of the Van Lake area is very similar to ssp *kocaki* and does not show the characters of ssp *karabagi*, therefore it is here included in the former, rather than in ssp *karabagi* as suggested by Hesselbarth et al. (1995)

RANGE
ssp *syriaca*: S. E. Turkey (Adana region), N. Syria
ssp *karabagi*: E. Turkey (Hakkari region)
ssp *kocaki*: S. E. Turkey

SELECTED REFERENCES
Hesselbarth et al. (1995), Koçak (1977)

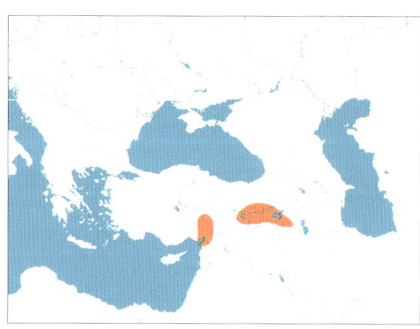

MELANARGIA OCCITANICA (Esper, 1793)

♂ ups   ♂ ups   ♀ ups   ♀ ups

♂ uns   ♂ uns   ♀ uns   ♀ uns

ssp *occitanica*
Mortola, Italy

ssp *occitanica*
Capo Mele, Italy

ssp *occitanica*
Capo Mele, Italy

ssp *occitanica*
Mortola, Italy

♂ ups   ♂ ups   ♂ ups   ♀ ups

♂ uns   ♂ uns   ♂ uns   ♀ uns

ssp *pelagia*
Taghzeft, M. Atlas, Morocco

ssp *pherusa*
S. Vito Lo Capo, Sicily

ssp *pherusa*
S. Vito Lo Capo, Sicily

ssp *pherusa*
S. Vito Lo Capo, Sicily

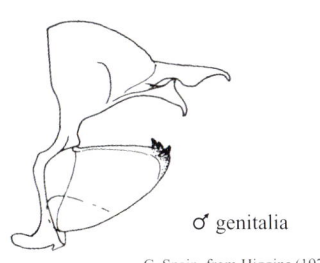

♂ genitalia

C. Spain, from Higgins (1975)

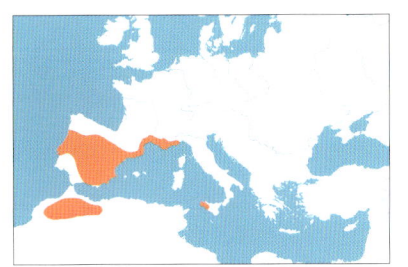

Papilio arge occitanica Esper, 1793, Schmett.
Abb. Nat. 1: 2
Type locality: Spain
- *claudiana* Merceron, 1998, Bull. Soc.
en. Mulhouse 1998: 15
- *pseudojapygia* de Sagarra, 1916, Butll.
Inst. catal. Hist. nat. 16: 77
- *psyche* Hübner, 1805, Sammlung Europ.
Schmett. 1 pl. 44 fig. 198-199
- *syllius* Herbst, 1796, Natursystem
Schmetterlinge 8: 15
Extensive lists of synonyms and individual
forms can be found in Gaede (1931),
Oberthür (1911) and Verity (1953)

DIAGNOSTIC CHARACTERS
upf broad black bar crossing the cell (a);
uph submarginal blue-pupilled ocelli (except
in ssp *pherusa*);
unh marginal chevrons acute-angled (b)
(obtuse-angled in *M. ines*, right-angled in
M. arge);
unh veins lined brown (lined black in *M. ines*
and *M. arge*);
unh longitudinal brown line in space 1b (c)
(absent in *M. ines*)

VARIATION
uph sometimes with an additional submarginal
ocellus in space 5;
uns ground colour variable from white to
creamy-yellow

ssp *pelagia* Oberthür, 1911
Melanargia syllius pelagia Oberthür, 1911,
Etud. Lep. comp. 5: 188
Type locality: Geryville [Skikda, Algeria]
- *megalatlasica* Tarrier, 1995, Alexanor
19: 204
- *moghrebiana* Varin, 1950, Revue fr.
Lép. 12: 341
upf base of space 3 white (usually darkened
in nominal *occitanica*) (d);
upf black bar crossing the cell closer to wing
base than in nominal *occitanica* and separated
from discal markings (e)

ssp *pherusa* Boisduval, 1832
Arge pherusa Boisduval, 1832, Icones pl. 26 fig. 4-6
Type locality: Sicily
usually smaller than nominal *occitanica*;
upf base of space 3 white (usually darkened
in nominal *occitanica*) (d);
upf black bar crossing the cell closer to wing
base than in nominal *occitanica* and separated
from discal markings (e);
uph black markings reduced, submarginal
ocelli absent or very small;
unh brown veins thinner than in nominal
occitanica and in ssp *pelagia*

TAXONOMIC NOTE
In N. Africa there is a clinal change from
West to East: specimens from Morocco are
very close to the nominal form, while in
Algeria ups markings are reduced almost as
in ssp *pherusa*.
Taxon *pherusa* is graded by some authors as
a good species on the basis of morphological
differences found in the early stages. Also
enzyme electrophoresis [Mensi et al. (1990)]
shows a significant genetic divergence
between taxa *occitanica* and *pherusa*

RANGE
ssp *occitanica*: Portugal, Spain, S. France, N.
W. Italy, Corsica ?
ssp *pelagia*: Morocco, W. Algeria
ssp *pherusa*: W. Sicily

SELECTED REFERENCES
Gaede (1939), Gomez Bustillo & Fernandez-
Rubio (1974), Jutzeler et al. (1996), Tarrier
(1995)

MELANARGIA INES (Hoffmannsegg, 1804)

♂ ups   ♀ ups

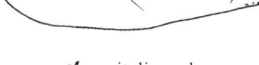

♂ uns   ♀ uns

Tafraoute, Anti Atlas, Morocco   Ketama, Rif, Morocco

♂ genitalia: valva
S. Spain, from Higgins (1975)

Papilio ines Hoffmannsegg, 1804, Ill. Mag. 3: 205
Type locality: Calabria (error for Cantabria) [Spain]
  – *arahoui* Tarrier, 1995, Alexanor 19: 206
  – *colossea* Rothschild, 1917, Novit. zool. 24: 111
  – *fathme* Wagner, 1913, Int. ent. Z. 7: 111
  – *henrike* Eitschberger, 1971, Ent. Z. Frankfurt 81: 145
  – *jahandiezi* Oberthür, 1922, Etud. Lép. comp. 19: 80
  – *thetis* Hübner, 1798, Samml. Eur. Schmett. pl. 47 fig. 196-197
  Extensive lists of synonyms and individual forms can be found in Gaede (1931) and Tennent (1996)

DIAGNOSTIC CHARACTERS
upf broad black bar crossing the cell (a);
uph submarginal blue-pupilled ocelli;
unh marginal chevrons obtuse-angled (b) (acute-angled in *M. occitanica*, right-angled in *M. arge*);
unh veins black (brown in *M. occitanica*);
unh without longitudinal line in space 1b (c) (a longitudinal brown line is present in *M. occitanica* and in *M. arge*)

VARIATION
Size varies considerably in all the colonies, small specimens are usual in arid areas.
The development of the black markings is variable: specimens with ups black markings heavier are frequent in the Madrid area and at high altitudes in the Moroccan Middle and High Atlas; specimens with reduced black markings and small submarginal ocelli are common at low altitudes in N. Africa and in S. W. Spain

RANGE
Spain, Portugal, Morocco, Algeria, Tunisia, Libya

SELECTED REFERENCES
Eitschberger (1971), Fernandez-Rubio (1991), Gaede (1939), Gomez Bustillo & Fernandez-Rubio (1974), Tennent (1996)

MELANARGIA ARGE (Sulzer, 1776)

♂ ups   ♂ ups   ♀ ups

♂ uns   ♂ uns   ♀ uns

Terni, Umbria, Italy   Salerno, Campania, Italy   Terni, Umbria, Italy

♂ genitalia: valva
C. Italy, from Higgins (1975)

Papilio arge Sulzer, 1776, Abgek. Geschichte der Insect.: 144
Type locality: Sicily [S. Italy]
  – *amphitrite* Hübner, 1799, Eur. Schmett. 1: 32
  – *cocuzzana* Stauder, 1914, Z. wiss. InsektBiol. 10: 375
  – *turatii* Rostagno, 1909, Boll. Soc. zool. ital. 7-8: 233
  Extensive lists of synonyms and individual forms can be found in Gaede (1931) and Verity (1953)

DIAGNOSTIC CHARACTERS
similar to *M. occitanica pherusa* and to *M. ines*, but:
upf black bar across cell incomplete (a);
unh veins lined black or dark brown;
unh submarginal ocelli large and prominent;
unh marginal chevrons right-angled (b) (obtuse-angled in *M. ines*, acute-angled in *M. occitanica*);
unh longitudinal curved dark line in space 1b (c) (absent in *M. ines*)

VARIATION
dark markings and submarginal ocelli reduced in f. *cocuzzana* and further reduced in f. *turatii*

RANGE
C. and S. Italy, N. E. Sicily

SELECTED REFERENCES
Russo (1996), Verity (1953)

MELANARGIA RUSSIAE (Esper, 1783)

σ ups — σ ups — σ ups — ♀ ups

σ uns — σ uns — σ uns — ♀ uns

| ssp *russiae* | ssp *russiae* | ssp *russiae* | ssp *russiae* |
| Kuragyno, E. Sayan Mts., S. Siberia | Kuragyno, E. Sayan Mts., S. Siberia | Palandoken, Erzurum, E. Turkey | Mt. Elbrus, Caucasus |

σ ups — σ ups — σ ups — ♀ ups

σ uns — σ uns — σ uns — ♀ uns

| ssp *russiae* "transcaspica" Turkmenistan | ssp *cleanthe* Mt. Louis, Pyrenees Or., France | ssp *cleanthe* Mont. de Lure, France | ssp *cleanthe* Mont. de Lure, France |

Papilio russiae Esper, 1783, Schmett. Abb. Nat. 1: 162
Type locality: S. Russia [from Sevastianovka to Penza, Russia]
– *caucasica* Nordmann, 1851 **syn. nov.**
Arge herta caucasica Nordmann, 1851, Bull. Soc. imp. Nat. Moscou 24: 403
taxon *caucasica* seems not to show any significant diagnostic character. Seitz (1911) quotes the very light uph discal band including white areas, but this character is found also in specimens of nominal *russiae* and it is not quoted either in the original description of *caucasica*, or in Wagener's (1975) review
– *clotho* Hübner, 1799, Sammlung Europ. Schmett. 1: 31
– *suwarovius* Herbst, 1796, Natur. Insekten 8: 13
– *transcaspica* Staudinger, 1901 **syn. nov.**
Melanargia japygia transcaspica Staudinger, 1901, in Staudinger & Rebel, Catal. Lep. Pal. Faun. 1: 41
taxon *transcaspica*, described as slightly smaller and darker than *suwarovius* (= *russiae*), does not show any diagnostic character justifying a subspecific rank
– *xenia* Freyer, 1845, Neu. Beitr. 6: 133
Extensive lists of synonyms and individual forms can be found in Gaede (1931) and Verity (1953)

DIAGNOSTIC CHARACTERS
upf transverse irregular black bar crossing the cell (a);
uph black circumcellular discal band (b) (absent in *M. parce*)

VARIATION
size variable;
dark suffusion and black markings variable, usually heavier in ssp *japygia* and *eberti*

ssp *cleanthe* Boisduval, 1833
Arge cleanthe Boisduval, 1833, Icon. 1: 139
Type locality: Basses Alpes
ups black markings well developed;
fw, both sides, large rectangular black spot in space 3 (c) (not constant)

19

♂ ups   ♀ ups   ♂ ups   ♀ ups

♂ uns   ♀ uns   ♂ uns   ♀ uns

| ssp *japygia* | ssp *japygia* | ssp *japygia* | ssp *japygia* |
| Gran Sasso, Abruzzo, Italy | Gran Sasso, Abruzzo, Italy | Madonie, Sicily, Italy | Madonie, Sicily, Italy |

♂ ups   ♀ ups

♂ uns   ♀ uns

ssp *eberti*   ssp *eberti*

Damavand, Iran   Damavand, Iran

♂ genitalia
ssp *japygia*
Baba Mt., Pelister, Macedonia
from Jaksic (1998)

ssp *japygia* Cyrillo, 1787
Papilio japygia Cyrillo, 1787, Entomol. Neapol. pl. 3 fig. 5
Type locality: Naples region
    – *atropos* Hübner, 1798, Sammlung Europ. Schmett. 1 fig. 192-193
    – *medioitalica* Verity, 1913, Boll. Soc. ent. ital. 45: 216
dark suffusion and black markings usually more pronounced than in the above subspecies;
fw, both sides, discal black marking in space 3 separated from cell-end by a white area (d) (not constant)

ssp *eberti* Wagener, 1975
Melanargia russiae eberti Wagener, 1975, J. ent. Soc. Iran Suppl. 1: 50
Type locality: Damavand, Polur, Masandaran, Elburs Mts., N. Iran
large;
dark suffusion and black markings well pronounced;
upf large rectangular black spot in space 3 (e) (same as in ssp *cleanthe*);
unf discal black marking in space 3 separated from cell-end by a grey-white area (f) (unlike ssp *cleanthe*)

TAXONOMIC NOTE
The status of taxon *japygia* seems questionable because of the variability of its diagnostic characters

RANGE
ssp *russiae*: S. Urals, E. Turkey, Caucasus, N. E. Iran, Turkmenistan, N. W. Tian Shan, Altai, W. Siberia, Sayan Mts.
ssp *cleanthe*: N. Portugal, N. and C. Spain, S. France
ssp *japygia*: C. and S. Italy, Balkans from Albania to N. Greece
ssp *eberti*: N. Iran

SELECTED REFERENCES
Gomez Bustillo & Fernandez-Rubio (1974), Verity (1953), Wagener (1975), Wagener (1980a)

MELANARGIA PARCE Staudinger, 1882

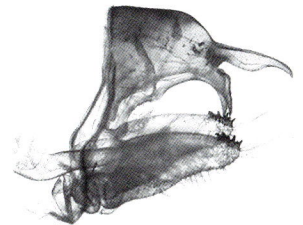

σ ups   σ ups   ♀ ups

σ uns   σ uns   ♀ uns

f. *lucida*   Namagan   Alai
Karategine, Atschik M.

σ genitalia
Alma Ata, Kazachstan

Melanargia parce Staudinger, 1882, Berl. ent. Z. 26: 170
Type locality: Margelan, Samarkand (Urgut), Hazret-Sultan Gebirge [Uzbekistan]
  – *fergana* Oberthür & Houlbert, 1922, C. r. hebd. Séanc. Acad. Sci. 174: 192
  – *lucida* Staudinger, 1886, Stettin. ent. Ztg. 47: 236
  – *persa* Grum-Grshimailo, 1890, in Romanoff Mém. Lép. 4: 441

DIAGNOSTIC CHARACTERS
upf transverse irregular black bar crossing the cell convex and less pronounced than in *M. russiae* (a); uph circumcellular discal band formed by black lines enclosing white areas (b) (the band is grey-black in *M. russiae*)

VARIATION
ups dark suffusion and black markings variable; ligth specimens, described as form *lucida*, are common

RANGE
S. E. Kazakhstan, E. Uzbekistan, E. Turkmenistan, N. Tadjikistan, Kirghizia,

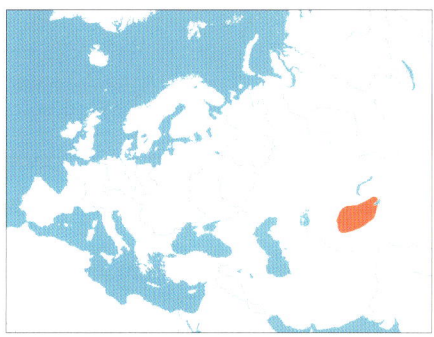

MELANARGIA LEDA Leech, 1891

♂ ups

b

c

♂ uns

ssp _leda_
Xinduqiao, W. Sichuan

♀ ups

♀ uns

ssp _leda_
Xinduqiao, W. Sichuan

♂ ups

♂ uns

ssp _yunnana_
Zhongdian, N. Yunnan

♀ ups

♀ uns

ssp _yunnana_
Likiang, N. Yunnan

a

♂ genitalia
from Wagener (1959)

a

♂ valva
Ta-pin-tze
from Wagener (1959)

Melanargia leda Leech, 1891, Entomologist suppl.: 57
Type locality: How-kow, Thibet [Yajiang, W. Sichuan, China]

DIAGNOSTIC CHARACTERS
male genitalia: valve with many apical teeth (a); smaller than all other Far East _Melanargia_ species;
upf black markings well developed, encircling two white spots in spaces 2 and 3 (b);
uph white submarginal chevrons acute-angled or square-angled (c);
uns dark markings suffused with yellow-green

VARIATION
ssp _yunnana_ Oberthür, 1891
Arge yunnana Oberthür, 1891, Etud. ent. 15: 13
Type locality: Hee-Chan-Men [N. Yunnan]
unh submarginal markings well developed

ssp _melli_ Wagener, 1961
Melanargia leda melli Wagener, 1961, Monogr. ostasiatischen Melanargia 3: 144
Type locality: Shiushekfut, W. Yunnan
unf submarginal markings ochreous-yellow

TAXONOMIC NOTE
The status of taxa _yunnana_ and _melli_ seems questionable because of the haziness of their diagnostic characters

RANGE
ssp _leda_: W. Sichuan
ssp _yunnana_: N. Yunnan
ssp _melli_: N. W. Yunnan

SELECTED REFERENCES
Houlbert (1922); Wagener (1959-1961)

MELANARGIA HALIMEDE (Ménétriés, 1858)

σ ups

♀ ups

upf
M. halimede

σ uns
ssp *halimede*
Donies, Amurland

♀ uns
ssp *halimede*
Chingan Mts., Pompejefka

upf
M. epimede and *M. ganymedes*
from Houlbert (1922)

σ valva
ssp *halimede*
Posiette Bay
from Wagener (1959)

σ genitalia
ssp *gratiani*
Maijishan, S. Gansu, China

σ ups

σ ups

σ ups

σ ups

σ uns
ssp *halimedina*
Korniloff, Korea

σ uns
ssp *coreana*
Port Hamilton, Korea

σ uns
ssp *coreana*
trans ad *"chosenica"*
Gensan, Korea

σ uns
ssp *coreana*
from *"chosenica"* range
Pyong-Yang, Korea

Arge halimede Ménétriés, 1858, Bull. phys. Acad. St. Petersbourg 17: 216
Type locality: Boureia Mts. up to Chome and Amour banks after the Ssoungary confluence [Amur region, Russia]
– *menetriesi* Houlbert, 1922, Etud. Lep. comp. 19 (2): 142

DIAGNOSTIC CHARACTERS
male genitalia valva with apical teeth arranged in two rows (a);
male genitalia distance between valva end and hollow end about a half than in *M. epimede*, *M. ganymedes* and *M. asiatica* (b);
fw apex pointed (rounded in *M. epimede* and *M. meridionalis*);
ups ground colour yellowish-white (pure white in *M. epimede*);
upf costal area in space 12 with a white suffusion (c) (not constant);
upf horizontal black bar along dorsum confined to space 1a and half of space 1b (d);
upf angle of the postdiscal band smaller than 120° (e);
upf submarginal white spot in space 1b large (f) (small or absent in *M. epimede*);
unh submarginal white lunules very wide (g);
unh discal dark line evident from costa to space 1 (h)

VARIATION
extension of black markings variable

ssp *halimedina* Bryk, 1947
Melanargia halimede halimedina Bryk, 1947, Ark. Zool. 38A (3): 27
Type locality: Motojondo [Korea]
– *sirojanome* Kishida, 1933, Kontyu 9: 43

ups submarginal dark suffusion more developed than in nominal *halimede* and usually covering the submarginal white spots;
upf black discal band less evident than in nominal *halimede*

ssp coreana Okamoto, 1926
Melanargia halimede coreana Okamoto, 1926, Zool. Mag. 38: 175
Type locality: South Korea
– *coreana* Sheljuzhko, 1929, Ent. Anz. 9: 49
– *chosenica* Wagener, 1961 **syn. nov.**
Melanargia halimede chosenica Wagener, 1961, Monogr. ostasiatischen Melanargia 3: 150
the populations from North-West Korea, described as ssp *coreana* by Sheljuzhko and subsequently renamed *chosenica* by Wagener, show dark markings usually less pronounced than in ssp *coreana* sensu Okamoto, but the variability of the dark markings found in all the range of *M. halimede* and the presence in Central Korea of populations with intermediate characters, suggest to keep only one subspecies inhabiting N.-W, Central and S. Korea
large;
upf dark submarginal suffusion more developed than in nominal *halimede* and usually covering the submarginal white spots;
male unh discal band well pronounced (i)

♂ ups   ♂ ups   ♀ ups

♂ uns   ♂ uns   ♀ uns

ssp *gratiani*
Min Shan or., Gansu mer.

ssp *gratiani* from
"*beicki*" range
Lanchowfu, Gansu

ssp *gratiani* from
"*beicki*" range
Gansu

ssp *gratiani* Wagener, 1961
Melanargia halimede gratiani Wagener, 1961,
Monogr. ostasiatischen Melanargia 3: 153
Type locality: Hsiho Ngan shan, Kansu mer.
[Gansu, China]

    – *beicki* Wagener, 1959 **syn. nov.**
    Melanargia halimede beicki Wagener,
    1959, Monogr. ostasiatischen Melanargia
    3: 153

    the variability and the haziness of
    the supposed diagnostic characters of
    taxon *beicki* do not to justify the rank
    of subspecies

ups dark submarginal suffusion more
developed than in nominal *halimede,* like
in ssp *coreana*;
upf black discal band well developed (a);
male unh discal band little pronounced, as in
nominal *halimede* and unlike ssp *coreana*

RANGE
ssp *halimede*: E. Mongolia, Amur and Ussuri
regions, N. E. China
ssp *halimedina*: N. E. Korea
ssp *coreana*: Korea
ssp *gratiani*: E. Qinghai, S. Gansu, Shaanxi
(China)

SELECTED REFERENCES
Houlbert (1922); Wagener (1959-1961)

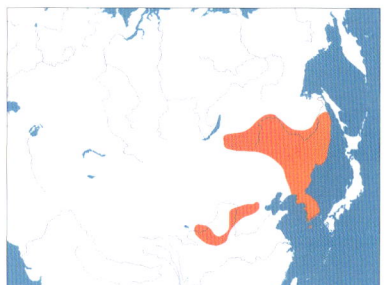

MELANARGIA MERIDIONALIS (Felder C. & R., 1862)

σ ups σ ups σ ups σ ups

σ uns σ uns σ uns σ uns

light form = nominal *meridionalis*
Zhuqu, S. Gansu, 104° 16' E.

f. *tsinica*
Wudu, S. Gansu, 105° 06' E.

f. *tsinica* trans ad *tapaishanensis*
Miaotaizi, W. Qin Ling 106° 46' E.

f. *tapaishanensis*
150 km S.-W. of Xi'an, Qin Ling 108° 26' E.

♀ ups ♀ ups σ ups

♀ uns ♀ uns σ uns

f. *tsinica*
Wudu, S. Gansu, 105° 06' E.

f. *tapaishanensis*
Qin Ling, 108° 50' E.

f. *fuscissima*
Pingli, Daba Shan, 109° 16' E..

σ ups σ uns

"*maritima*"
Chusan I.

σ ups σ uns

"*wenchowensis*"
Wenchow (Chekiang)

Melanargia halimede meridionalis Felder C. & R., 1862, Wien ent. Monats. 6: 29
Type locality: Ning Po [Ningbo, Zhejiang, China]

– *fuscissima* Houlbert, 1922, Etud. Lep. 19: 132 name given to the completely dark form, misinterpreted as a good species by its author

– *maritima* Wagener, 1961 **syn. nov.**
Melanargia meridionalis maritima Wagener, 1961, Monogr. ostasiatischen Melanargia 3: 154
taxon *maritima*, described as slightly smaller and lighter than nominal *meridionalis*, does not show any reliable diagnostic character justifying a subspecific rank

– *tapaishanensis* Wagener, 1961 **syn. nov.**
Melanargia meridionalis tapaishanensis Wagener, 1961, Monogr. ostasiatischen Melanargia 3: 156

– *tsinica* Wagener, 1961 **syn. nov.**
Melanargia meridionalis tsinica Wagener, 1961, Monogr. ostasiatischen Melanargia 3: 156

– *wenchowensis* Wagener, 1961 **syn. nov.**
Melanargia meridionalis wenchowensis Wagener, 1961, Monogr. ostasiatischen Melanargia 3: 155
see under VARIATION

DIAGNOSTIC CHARACTERS
male genitalia: valva smaller than in *M. lugens*;
male genitalia distance between valva end and hollow end about a half than in *M. epimede, M. ganymedes* and *M. asiatica* (e);
fw apex rounded (pointed in *M. halimede*);
fw outer margin more rounded than in *M. halimede*;
upf black suffusion in the costal area of the cell almost reaching wing base (a)
upf horizontal black bar along dorsum covering almost completely space 1b (less extended in *M. lugens*);
upf angle of the postdiscal band about 130° (b) (larger than 150° in *M. lugens*);
uns ground colour white-yellowish (pure white in the light forms of *M. lugens*);
uns submarginal white chevrons narrower than in *M. lugens* (c);
uns ground colour yellow (white or white-yellowish in *M. lugens*)

VARIATION
M. meridionalis is known from the coastal area in Zhejiang and Fujian regions and from the mountains in S. Shaanxi and S. Gansu.
The two areas are 1200 kilometres away and no specimens seem to be available from the Hubei and Anhui regions, that are between them.
In both areas *meridionalis* is represented by populations ranging from strongly melanic to more or less light.
Within a single population the morphological characters are quite constant, but in the S. Gansu - S. Shaanxi range, where many specimens have been recently collected, it takes place a cline ranging from the light nominal *meridionalis* form (West of Min Shan in S. Gansu at a longitude of 104° East), to the darker *tsinica* form (in Min Shan and Peiling Shan at a longitude of 105° East), to an even darker form (in Western Qin Ling at a longitude of 106° East) and to the extremely dark *tapaishanensis* form (in Central and Eastern Qin Ling and in Daba Shan in S.-E. Shaanxi at a longitude of 107°-108° East).
In the Southern part of the Zhejiang - Fujian area it is found the dark form *wenchowensis*, almost reaching the degree of melanism of *tapaishanensis*, while the Northern part of the area is inhabited by the light nominal form. It seems predictable that further researches in the area will produce populations with intermediate characters.
All the previously named subspecies have therefore to be ranked as clinal forms.

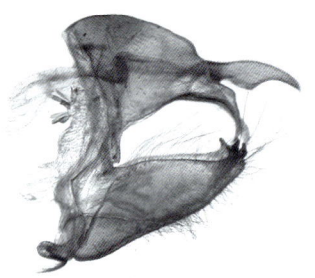

♂ genitalia
Qin Ling, Shaanxi

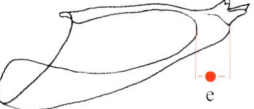

♂ genitalia: valva
Tapaishan
from Wagener (1959)

RANGE
S. Gansu, S. Shaanxi, E. Zhejiang and E. Fujian (China)

SELECTED REFERENCES
Houlbert (1922); Wagener (1959-1961)

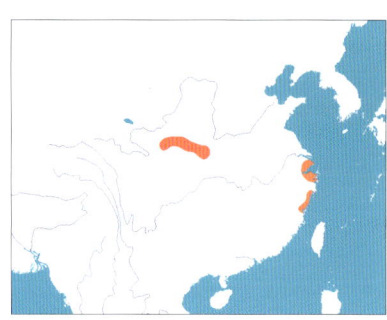

MELANARGIA MONTANA (Leech, 1890)

● b

♂ ups

♂ ups

♀ ups

♂ uns
Chang Yang

♂ uns
Chang Yang
● c

♀ uns
Chang Yang

♂ ups
"chloris"
PARATYPE BMNH
Kwanshien

♂ ups
"clarens"
Maijishan, S. Gansu

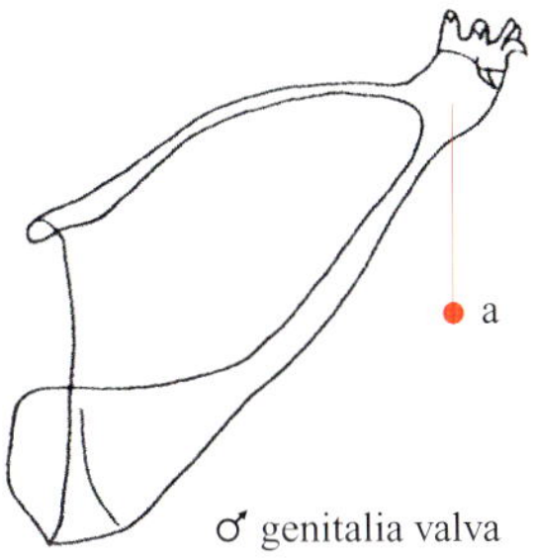

♂ genitalia valva
Chang Yang
from Wagener (1959)
● a

♂ ups
Zhouzhi, Shaanxi

♂ ups
Hanyin, QinLing Mts., Shaanxi

♂ ups
Hanyin, QinLing Mts., Shaanxi

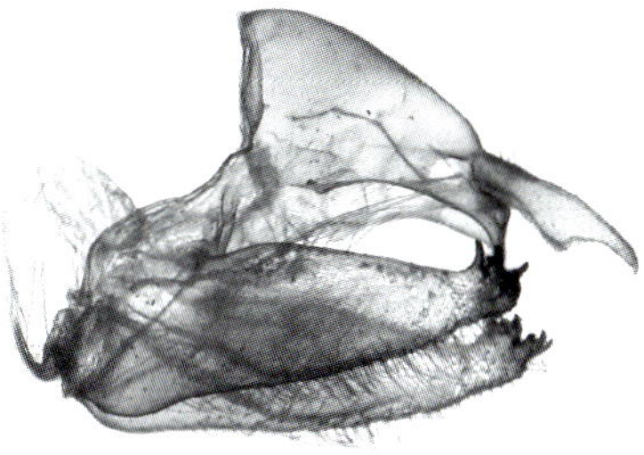

"clarens"
♂ genitalia
Maijishan, S. Gansu

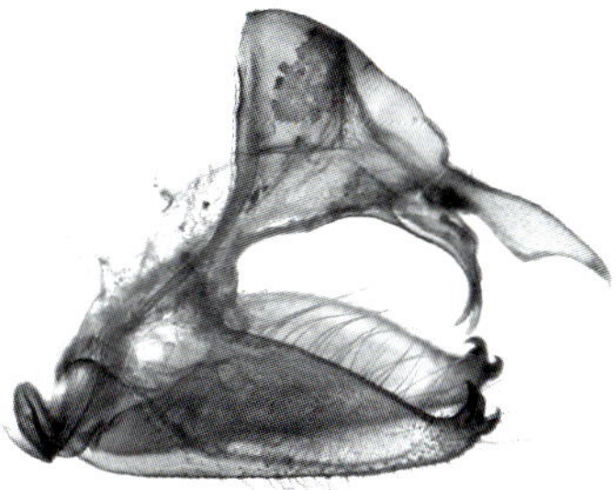

♂ genitalia
Luohe Daba Shan, Shaanxi

Melanargia halimede montana Leech, 1890,
Entomologist 23: 26
Type locality: Chang Yang [Changyang,
Hubei, China]
   – *chloris* Wagener, 1961 **syn. nov.**
   Melanargia montana chloris Wagener,
1961, Monogr. ostasiatischen Melanargia
3: 158
   the large size and upf larger angle
of the posdiscal band (b), quoted as
diagnostic characters for ssp *chloris*
from W. Sichuan, are often found also
in nominal *montana*
   – *clarens* Wagener, 1961 **syn. nov.**
   Melanargia lugens clarens Wagener,
1961, Monogr. ostasiatischen Melanargia
3: 158
   taxon *clarens*, described from S. Gansu
as a subspecies of *lugens*, shows partially
developed black markings and has the
small size of *lugens*, but both characters
are frequently found in Shaanxi
populations of *montana*; its distribution
range is inside that of *montana,* far away
from *lugens* range

DIAGNOSTIC CHARACTERS
male genitalia: valva longer than in all other
oriental species (except *M. lugens*), with distal
part long and slender (a);
fw apex and outer margin rounded;
upf angle of the postdiscal band larger than
150° (b);
all the above characters, except the shape of the
valva, apply also to *lugens*, but *montana* has:
size usually larger than *lugens*;
black markings usually very reduced, never
reaching the extension found in *lugens*

VARIATION
the size is generally much larger than in any
other *Melanargia* species, but in Shaanxi
and Gansu regions small specimens are
often found;
the black markings, extremely reduced in
the southern and eastern part of the range,
are more pronounced in the Shaanxi region,
where a mix of very light and quite dark
specimens are found flying together;
in the light specimens uph ocelli vary from
absent to evident;
unh size of the submarginal white chevrons
variable (c)

TAXONOMIC NOTE
Taxa *montana* and *lugens* could be
expressions of a cline produced by a single
species; their ranges seem not to overlap
and East Shaanxi populations show wing
markings intermediate between typical light
montana and typical dark *lugens*

RANGE
Hubei, Guizhou, S. Shaanxi, S. Gansu,
Sichuan

SELECTED REFERENCES
Wagener (1959-1961)

MELANARGIA LUGENS (Honrath, 1888)

♂ ups ♂ ups ♀ ups

♂ uns ♂ uns ♀ uns

ssp *lugens*
PARATYPE BMNH
Kiukiang

ssp *lugens*
PARATYPE BMNH
Kiukiang

ssp *lugens*
PARATYPE BMNH
Kiukiang

♂ ups ♂ ups ♀ ups ♂ ups

♂ uns ♂ uns ♀ uns ♂ uns

ssp *ahyoui*
PARATYPE BMNH
Mokanshan, Chekiang

ssp *hengshanensis*
HOLOTYPE ZFMK
Hoeng Shan, prov. Hunan

ssp *hengshanensis*
ALLOTYPE ZFMK
Hoeng Shan, prov. Hunan

ssp *hoenei*
PARATYPE BMNH
Nanking, Purple Mts.

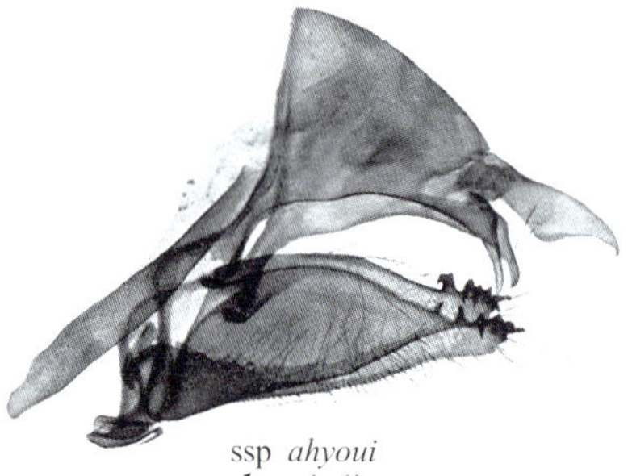

ssp *ahyoui*
♂ genitalia
Mokanshan, Chekiang
from Wagener (1959-1961)

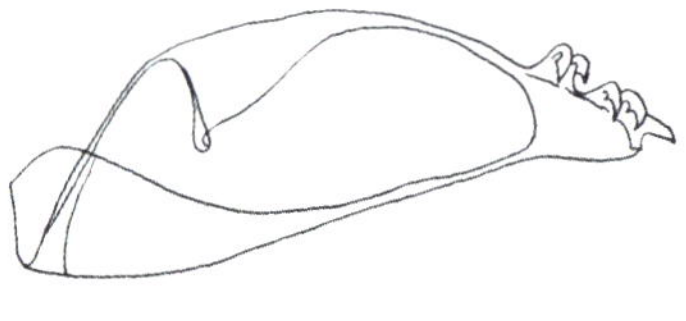

ssp *lugens*
♂ genitalia: valva
Kiukiang
from Wagener (1959-1961)

Melanargia halimede lugens Honrath, 1888, Ent. Nachr. 14: 161
Type locality: Kiukiang [Jiujiang, Jiangxi, China]

DIAGNOSTIC CHARACTERS
male genitalia: valva longer than in all other oriental species, except *M. montana*;
fw apex and outer margin rounded;
upf angle of the postdiscal band larger than 150° (a) (not constant);
all the above characters apply to *montana* also, but *lugens* has:
size usually smaller than *montana*;
ups black markings always well pronounced;
uns ground colour white or white-yellowish (more yellow in *M. meridionalis*)

VARIATION
ssp *ahyoui* Wagener, 1961
Melanargia lugens ahyoui Wagener, 1961, Monogr. ostasiatischen Melanargia 3: 159
Type locality: Mokanshan, prov. Chekiang [Mogan Shan, N. Zhejiang]
ups black suffusion less pronounced than in nominal *lugens*

ssp *hengshanensis* Wagener, 1961
Melanargia lugens hengshanensis Wagener, 1961, Monogr. ostasiatischen Melanargia 3: 159
Type locality: Hoeng-Shan, prov. Hunan [Hengyang, Hunan]
ups black suffusion less pronounced than in ssp *ahyoui*;
ups black marginal area narrower than in ssp *ahyoui*;
unh submarginal ocelli small (b)

ssp *hoenei* Wagener, 1961
Melanargia lugens hoenei Wagener, 1961, Monogr. ostasiatischen Melanargia 3: 158
Type locality: Nanking Purple Mountains [Nanjing, Anhui]
ups black suffusion less pronounced than in all the above ssp

TAXONOMIC NOTE
As pointed out by Wagener (1959-1961) it is possible that the above subspecies are part of a cline, same as in *M. meridionalis*. But, unlike *M. meridionalis*, no specimens showing intermediate characters between the subspecies are available, therefore, until new evidence, the rank of good subspecies should be maintained.
The specific distintion between *lugens* and *montana* is questionable (see Taxonomic Note under *M. montana*)

RANGE
ssp *lugens*: N. Jiangxi (China)
ssp *ahyoui*: Zhejiang (China)
ssp *hengshanensis*: Hunan (China)
ssp *hoenei*: Anhui (China)

SELECTED REFERENCES
Wagener (1959-1961)

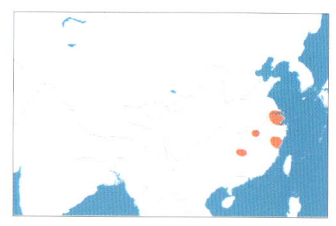

MELANARGIA EPIMEDE (Staudinger, 1887)

ssp *epimede*
Barabash, Far East Russia

ssp *epimede*
Zhang Guang Cai Shan,
Heilongjiang, N. E. China

ssp *epimede*
Ludao,
Heilongjiang, N. E. China

ssp *epimede* "corimede"
HOLOTYPE ZFMK
Umgebung Sei-Shin,
Nordkorea

ssp *epimede* "koreargia"
Sangdong, S. Korea

ssp *epimede* "pasiteles"
Shandong, China

ssp *pseudolugens*
HOLOTYPE ZFMK
Mienshan, prov. Shansi

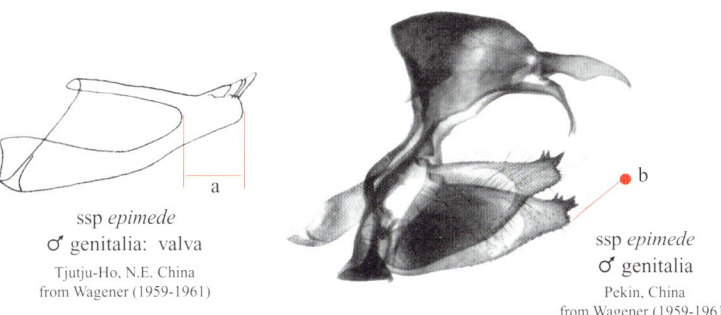

ssp *epimede*
♂ genitalia: valva
Tjutju-Ho, N.E. China
from Wagener (1959-1961)

ssp *epimede*
♂ genitalia
Pekin, China
from Wagener (1959-1961)

Melanargia halimede epimede Staudinger, 1887, in Romanoff Mem. Lep. 3: 147
Type locality: Raddefkaja [Radde, Amur reg., Russia]
– *corimede* Wagener, 1961, **syn. nov.**
Melanargia epimede corimede Wagener, 1961, Monogr. ostasiatischen Melanargia 3: 165
taxon *corimede* from N. Korea, was described as larger and darker than nominal *epimede*, but, as stated by Wagener in his description, it is linked to nominal *epimede* by populations showing intermediate characters and it seems to belong to a cline ranging from light forms usual in the Amur region to dark forms usual in S. Korea
– *koreargia* Bryk, 1946, **syn. nov.**
Melanargia halimede koreargia Bryk, 1946, Ark. Zool. 38A: 26
as stated above, taxon *koreargia* from S. Korea is the darkest form of the cline
– *hanlaensis* Okano & Pak, 1968, Artes Liberales 4: 65
– *pasiteles* Fruhstorfer, 1911, **syn. nov.**
Arge halimede pasiteles Fruhstorfer, 1911, in Seitz, Grossschmett. Erde 9: 310
taxon *pasiteles*, from the Shandong region in China, does not show any reliable diagnostic character sustaining a subspecific rank
– *mandjuriana* Houlbert, 1922, Etud. Lep. comp. 19 (2): 132
– *mureisana* Kishida, 1933, Lansania 4: 36

DIAGNOSTIC CHARACTERS
male genitalia: distance between end of valva and end of hollow almost double than in *M. halimede* and *M. meridionalis* (a);
valva with few and large apical teeth (not constant);
valva distal end with an angular protrusion below the teeth (b);
fw apex more rounded than in *M. halimede*;
ups ground colour pure white (yellowish-white in *M. halimede*);
upf costal area suffused with dark scales (c) (see under *M. halimede*);
upf black bar in space 1a and 1b wider than in *M. halimede* (d);
upf submarginal white spot in space 1b narrow or absent (e) (large in *M. halimede*);
uph submarginal white chevrons very narrow or completely covered with black (f) (well defined in *M. ganymedes*);
unh submarginal white chevrons narrow (g) (wide in *M. halimede*)

VARIATION
size variable;
extension of dark markings variable

ssp *pseudolugens* Forster, 1942
Melanargia meridionalis pseudolugens Forster, 1942, Ent. Zeit. 55: 217
Type locality: Mienshan [Taiyue Shan, Shanxi, China]
resembling the darkest forms of *M. meridionalis*, but showing the male genitalia characters of *M. epimede*

RANGE
ssp *epimede*: Amur, Ussuri, E. Mongolia, Korea, N. E. China
ssp *pseudolugens*: Shanxi (N. China)

SELECTED REFERENCES
Wagener (1959-1961)

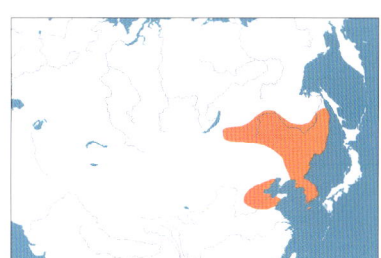

MELANARGIA GANYMEDES (Heyne, 1895)

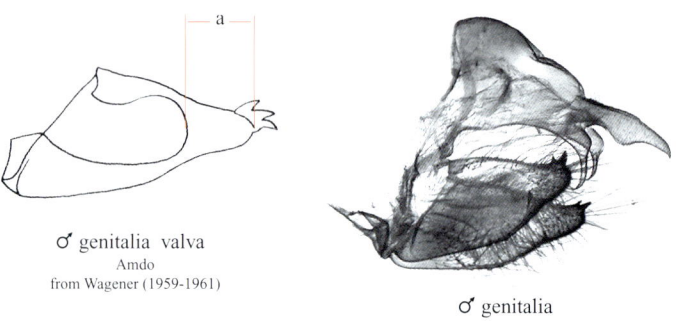

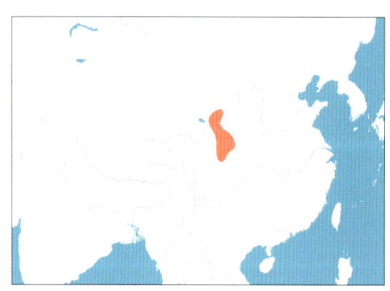

b

c

d

♂ ups

♀ ups

♂ ups

♂ uns
Huangyuan, Qinghai

♀ uns
Huangyuan, Qinghai

♂ uns
"walleseri"
Linxia, Gansu

♂ ups

♂ ups

♂ ups

♂ uns
"weigoldi"
Zhaga, Songpan, N. Sichuan

♂ uns
"weigoldi"
Wolong, Qionglai Shan, W. Sichuan

♂ uns
"weigoldi"
Jiuzhaigou, Songpan, N. Sichuan

a

♂ genitalia valva
Amdo
from Wagener (1959-1961)

♂ genitalia
Huangyuan, Qinghai

Melanargia epimede ganymedes Heyne, 1895, in Rühl & Bartel Pal. Grossschmett. Tagfalter 1: 804
Type locality: Kuku-noor [Qinghai, China]
– *walleseri* Wagener, 1961, **syn. nov.**
Melanargia ganymedes walleseri Wagener, 1961, Monogr. ostasiatischen Melanargia 3: 172
the populations from S. Gansu, described as subspecies *walleseri*, show well pronounced black markings, especially on upf apex and submarginal costal area, but this character is often found also in the nominal subspecies
– *weigoldi* Wagener, 1961, **syn. nov.**
Melanargia ganymedes weigoldi Wagener, 1961, Monogr. ostasiatischen Melanargia 3: 172
taxon *weigoldi*, from Songpan in N-W Sichuan and from the Qionglai Shan area in W. Sichuan, was described as being smaller than nominal *ganymedes*, but the analysys of large series shows that in populations from various areas around Songpan both the size and the development of the black markings are variable and that specimens not presenting any significant difference from nominal *ganymedes*, or even large and light, are not uncommon

DIAGNOSTIC CHARACTERS
male genitalia: distance between end of valva and end of hollow almost double than in *M. halimede* and *M. meridionalis* (a);
valva with few large apical teeth (not constant);
fw apex rounded;
upf costal area suffused with dark scales (b) (white or little suffused with dark scales in *M. asiatica*; see under *M. halimede*);
uph submarginal white chevrons well defined, narrow, but larger than in *M. epimede* (c);
unh submarginal white chevrons narrow (d)

VARIATION
male genitalia: shape of valva distal end variable;
size variable;
ups black lining of veins obsolete in some populations

TAXONOMIC NOTE
Separation of taxa *ganymedes* and *asiatica* is sometimes very difficult because of the haziness of their diagnostic characters. As stated by Wagener (1959-1961) the two taxa could belong to a single species complex

RANGE
Qinghai, C. and S. Gansu, N. and W. Sichuan (China)

SELECTED REFERENCES
Wagener (1959-1961)

MELANARGIA ASIATICA Oberthür & Houlbert, 1922

Melanargia asiatica Oberthür & Houlbert, 1922,
C. R. hebd. Seanc. Acad. Sci. 174: 190
Type locality: Ta-tsien-Lou [Kangding, Sichuan,
China]
> –*anophtalma* Draeseke, 1925, Deut. Ent. Zeit.
> [Iris] 39: 56
> – *armandi* Wagener, 1961, **syn. nov.**
> *Melanargia asiatica armandi* Wagener, 1961,
> Monogr. ostasiatischen Melanargia 3: 176
> taxon *armandi*, described from the area east
> of Kangding, was supposed to have upf black
> bar narrower than in nominal *asiatica* and
> uph veins strongly lined with black; however
> the populations from *armandi* range show
> very variable morphological characters and
> specimens identical to nominal *asiatica* are
> not uncommon
> – *yalongensis* Houlbert, 1922, Etud. Lep.
> comp. [Oberthür] 19 (2): 129

DIAGNOSTIC CHARACTERS
valva usually with more teeth than in *M. ganymedes*;
valva distal end rounded, without the angular
protrusion present in *M. epimede*;
fw apex rounded;
upf costal area white or little suffused with dark
scales (a);
uph submarginal white chevrons well defined,
narrow, but larger than in *M. epimede* (b);
unh submarginal white chevrons narrow (c)

VARIATION
size variable;
upf size and shape of black bar in space 1 variable

ssp *dejeani* Wagener, 1961
Melanargia asiatica dejeani Wagener, 1961,
Monogr. ostasiatischen Melanargia 3: 173
Type locality: Ta-tsien-Lou [W. of Kangding, Sichuan]
small;
ups black markings well developed;
upf black bar thick, covering almost completely
space 1b (d)

ssp *elisa* Wagener, 1961
Melanargia asiatica elisa Wagener, 1961, Monogr.
ostasiatischen Melanargia 3: 177
Type locality: Li-kiang [Lijiang, N. Yunnan]
large; ups black markings reduced;
upf black bar narrower than in ssp *asiatica* and
dejeani (f)

ssp *asiatica*	ssp *asiatica*	ssp *asiatica* "*armandi*"
10 km E. of Kangding, Sichuan	10 km E. of Kangding, Sichuan	180 km S.-W. of Chengdu, Sichuan

ssp *dejeani*	ssp *elisa*	ssp *elisa*
10 km S. of Kangding, Sichuan	Gazar, Zhongdian, Yunnan	Puloen, Zhongdian, Yunnan

♂ ups   b   ♀ ups
a
♂ uns   ♀ uns

ssp *wageneri*
PARATYPE
Yajiang, W. Sichuan

ssp *wageneri*
PARATYPE
Yajiang, W. Sichuan

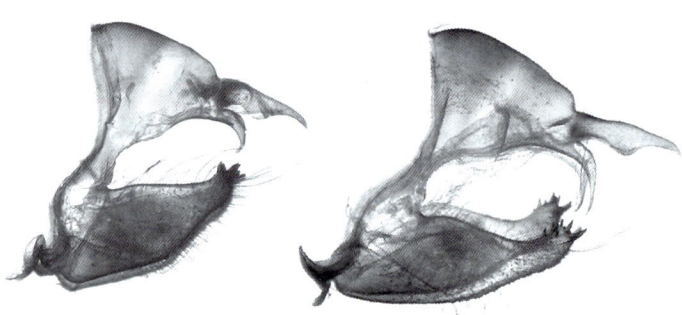

ssp *asiatica*
♂ genitalia
10 km E. of Kangding, Sichuan

ssp *wageneri*
♂ genitalia
Yajiang, W. Sichuan

ssp *wageneri* **ssp nov.**
Holotype: ♂ Yajiang m. 2700, W. Sichuan, China 19.VII.1992 leg. G.C. Bozano, deposited at the Koenig Museum, Bonn, Germany
Paratypes: 22 ♂, 1♀, same locality, in coll. Bozano, 10 ♂, same locality, in coll. Della Bruna;
the subspecies is named after Mr. Sigbert Wagener, doubtlessly the lepidopterist with the most extensive knowledge of the genus *Melanargia*;
ups black markings very reduced;
ups veins little outlined with black;
upf white submarginal lunules well defined (a) (covered by dark scales in all other subspecies);
upf postdiscal black marking in space 2 obsolete (b) (usually evident in all other subspecies);
upf black bar in space 1 very narrow;
female similar to male

TAXONOMIC NOTE
See under *M. ganymedes*

RANGE
ssp *asiatica*: W. and N. Sichuan; S. Gansu (China)
ssp *dejeani*: W. Sichuan, W. of the range of *asiatica*
ssp *wageneri*: W. Sichuan, W. of the range of *dejeani*
ssp *elisa*: N. Yunnan (China); N. Burma

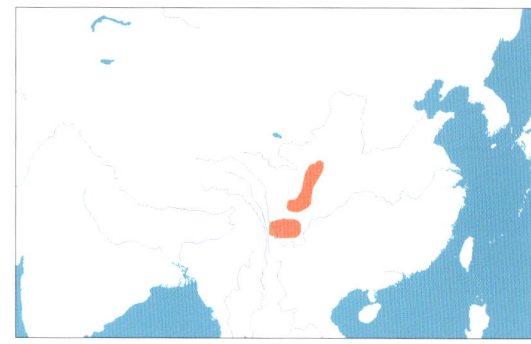

32

Subtribe **COENONYMPHINA** Miller, 1968

Coenonymphini Miller, 1968, Mem. amer. ent. Soc. 24: 95

DIAGNOSTIC CHARACTERS
Eyes naked;
antennae shorter than half the length of the forewing costa;
male foreleg weakly developed with unspined tarsus;
female foreleg reduced, with no more than four tarsal subsegments;
midtibia very long;
forewing cell deeply excavate;
forewing base of veins 1, subcostal and cubital inflated

TAXONOMIC NOTE
Genus *Aphantopus* previously included in the Subtribe Coenonymphina, is now attributed to the Subtribe Maniolina;
genus *Lyela* has also been removed from Subtribe Coenonymphina and its attribution seems so far uncertain.

CHECKLIST OF THE GENERA
Coenonympha Hübner, 1819
Sinonympha Lee, 1974
Triphysa Zeller, 1850

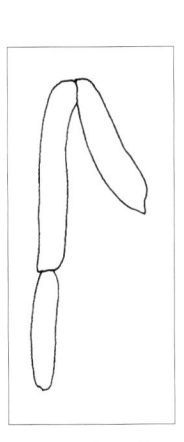

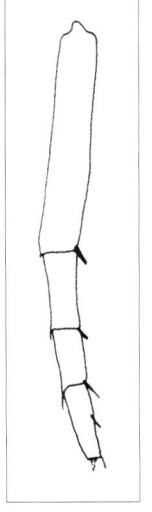

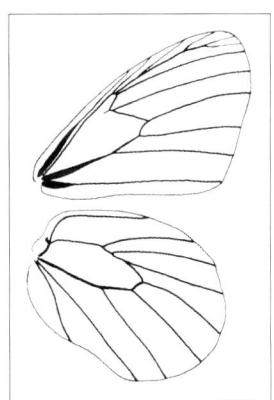

Coenonympha oedippus
♂ foreleg
from Miller (1968)

Coenonympha oedippus
♀ foreleg
from Miller (1968)

Coenonympha oedippus
♂ venation
from Miller (1968)

genus **COENONYMPHA** Hübner, 1819

Coenonympha Hübner, 1819, Verz. bekannt. Schmett. (5):65
Type species: *Papilio geticus* Esper, 1793 [= *Coenonympha oedippus* Fabricius, 1787]
   – *Chortobius* Dunning & Pickard, 1858, Accentuated List Brit. Lep.: 5
   – *Sicca* Verity, 1953, Le Farfalle Diurne d'Italia 5: 83

DIAGNOSTIC CHARACTERS
Eyes naked;
antennae short, not strongly clubbed;
palpi slender, rather long;
male genitalia: uncus longer than tegumen, falces slender and pointed, apex angularis well developed, valve slender and tapering, longer than tegumen plus uncus;
forewing base of veins 1, subcostal and cubital inflated;
hindwing precostal vein absent

RANGE
Holarctic, with two species (*C. tullia* and *C. haydenii*) found in the Nearctic region

SELECTED REFERENCES
Davenport (1941)

CHECKLIST OF THE SPECIES FOUND IN THE PALEARCTIC REGION

tullia tullia (Müller, 1764)
   tullia davus (Fabricius, 1777)
   tullia scotica (Staudinger, 1901)
   tullia demophyle (Freyer, 1844)
   tullia bosniae Davenport, 1941
   tullia chatiparae (Sheljuzhko, 1937)
   tullia caeca (Staudinger, 1901)
   tullia subcaeca (Heyne, 1894)
   tullia viluiensis (Ménétriés, 1859)
rhodopensis (Elwes, 1900)
glycerion glycerion (Borkhausen, 1788)
   glycerion bertolis (de Prunner, 1798)
   glycerion korshunovi Nekrutenko, 1978
   glycerion iphina (Staudinger, 1892)
   glycerion iphicles (Staudinger, 1892)
iphioides iphioides (Staudinger, 1870)
   iphioides pearsoni Romei, 1927
mahometana (Alphéraky, 1888)
sunbecca (Eversmann, 1843)
symphita Lederer, 1870
amaryllis amaryllis (Stoll, 1782)
   amaryllis pavonina Alphéraky, 1888
   amaryllis tydeus Leech, 1892
   amaryllis emmonsi Davenport, 1941
   amaryllis forsteri Gross, 1961
sinica Alphéraky, 1888
mangeri Bang-Haas, 1927
hero hero (Linnaeus, 1761)
   hero perseis Lederer, 1853
   hero latifasciata Matsumura, 1925
arcania arcania (Linnaeus, 1761)
gardetta gardetta (de Prunner, 1798)
   gardetta lecerfi de Lesse, 1949
   gardetta darwiniana Staudinger, 1871
orientalis (Rebel, 1910)
arcanioides (Pierret, 1837)
leander leander (Esper, 1784)
   leander dierli Koçak, 1977
   leander iranica Schwingenschuss, 1939
nolckeni Erschoff, 1874
mongolica Alphéraky, 1881

dorus dorus (Esper, 1782)
   dorus bieli Staudinger, 1901
   dorus cerratoi Rojio, 1997
fettigii fettigii Oberthür, 1874
   fettigii nicholasi (Rothschild, 1925)
austauti (Oberthür, 1881)
vaucheri vaucheri Blachier, 1905
   vaucheri annoceuri Wyatt, 1952
   vaucheri rifensis Weiss, 1979
   vaucheri beraberensis Lay & Rose, 1979
corinna corinna (Hübner, 1803)
   corinna trettaui Gross, 1970
elbana (Staudinger, 1901)
saadi saadi (Kollar, 1850)
   saadi mesopotamica Heyne, 1894
pamphilus (Linnaeus, 1758)
thyrsis (Freyer, 1845)
sunbecca (Eversmann, 1843)
semenovi semenovi Alphéraky, 1887
   semenovi leanotchka Hemming, 1933
   semenovi jiadengyuica Huang & Murayama, 1992
   semenovi sala Kocman, 1996
oedippus oedippus (Fabricius, 1787)

CHECKLIST OF THE SPECIES NOT FOUND IN THE PALEARCTIC REGION

tullia inornata Edwards, 1861
tullia benjamini McDunnough, 1928
tullia ochracea Edwards, 1861
tullia ampelos Edwards, 1871
tullia kodiak Edwards, 1869
tullia mackenziei Davenport, 1936
tullia california Westwood, 1851
haydenii Edwards, 1872

COENONYMPHA TULLIA (Müller, 1764)

a •

a •

b •

♂ ups   ♀ ups   ♂ ups   ♂ ups

♂ uns   ♀ uns   ♂ uns   ♂ uns

ssp *tullia*
Altmatt, Schwyz,
Switzerland

ssp *tullia*
Altmatt, Schwyz,
Switzerland

ssp *tullia*
Benderloch, Argyll,
England

ssp *tullia* "*fiori*"
Fusine, Friuli Venezia
Giulia, Italy

♂ ups   ♀ ups   ♂ ups

♂ uns   ♀ uns   ♂ uns

ssp *davus*
Nicholls Wodds,
Witherslack, Cumbria

ssp *davus*
Nicholls Wodds,
Witherslack, Cumbria

ssp *scotica*
from Emmeth & Heath
(1989)

♂ ups   ♂ ups   ♂ ups

♂ uns   ♂ uns   ♂ uns

ssp *demophile*
Avesta, C. Sweden

ssp *chatiparae*
Yatirgvarta, W. Caucasus

ssp *viluiensis*
Yakutsk, Botanicheskiy sad,
Yakutia, Russia

Papilio tullia Müller, 1764, F. Ins. Frid.: 36
Type locality: Frederiksdal, Denmark
   – *fiori* Verity, 1953, Farf. Diurn. Italia 5: 123
   – *laidion* Borkhausen, 1788, Eur. Schmett. 1: 91
   – *polydama* Haworth, 1828, Lepid. Brit.: 16
   – *philoxenoides* Schawerda, 1909, Jber. Wien. ent. Ver. 19: 85
   – *philoxenus* Esper, 1780, Schmett. 1 t. 54 f. 3
   – *tiphon* Rottemburg, 1775, Naturf. 6: 15
   – *typhon* Kirby, 1871, Syn. Catal. Diurn. Lep. 1: 99

DIAGNOSTIC CHARACTERS
unf with a whitish postdiscal line (a);
the separation from *C. amaryllis* is usually very easy through the following characters:
unh submarginal silver line absent in *C. tullia*;
unf postdiscal dark line absent in *C. tullia*;
unh shape of the postdiscal white spot (b)

VARIATION
very variable, locally and individually, in:
size;
ups and uns development of submarginal ocelli;
ups ground colour;
unh size and shape of the white postdiscal spot

ssp *davus* Fabricius, 1777
Papilio davus Fabricius, 1777, Ge. Ins.: 259
Type locality: Hamburg, Germany
   – *rothliebii* Herrich-Schäffer, Syst. Bearb. Schmett. Europa 6: 18
ups darker grey-brown than in nominal *tullia*;
unh ground colour grey-brown;
unh submarginal ocelli more developed than in nominal *tullia*;
unh postdiscal white band more developed than in nominal *tullia*

ssp *scotica* Staudinger, 1901
Coenonympha tiphon scotica Staudinger, 1901, in Staudinger & Rebel Catal. Lep. Pal. Fauna: 66
Type locality: Scotland
ups pale yellow-brown with whitish shading at the margins (not present in ssp *demophile*);
unh submarginal ocelli small or obsolete;
unh grey

ssp *demophile* Freyer, 1844
Hipparchia demophile Freyer, 1844, Neue. Beitr. Schmett. Abb. Nat. 5: 97 t. 439 f. 3, 4
Type locality: Lapland
   – *isis* Becklin, 1791, in Thunberg Diss. Ent. sist. Ins. Svecica 2: 31
   – *orstadii* Wahlgren, 1930, Svensk Insektfauna 10: 1
   – *suevica* Hemming, 1936, Proc. R. ent. Soc. Lond. 5: 123
uns ocellation very reduced or absent;
replaced in the far north by subspecies *viluiensis*, greysh above and below

ssp *bosniae* Davenport, 1941
Coenonympha tullia bosniae Davenport, 1941, Bull. Harvard Mus. Comp. Zool. 87: 244
Type locality: Lake Jesero, Bosnia
   – *lorkovici* Sijaric & Carnelutti, 1976, Wiss. Mitt. bosn.-herzeg. Landesmus. 6: 179
large;
ups and uns dark as in ssp *davus*;
uns ocelli well developed

ssp *chatiparae* Sheljuzhko, 1937
Coenonympha tiphon chatiparae Sheljuzhko, 1937, Festschrift Prof. E. Strand 2: 353
Type locality: Teberda, Chatipara Mts., Nord-Kaukasus
very similar to ssp *demophile*, but ups lighter brown

ssp *viluiensis* Ménétriés, 1859
Coenonympha isis viluiensis Ménétriés, 1859, in Schrenk, Reisen im Amur-Lande 2(1): 44
Type locality: riv. Viloui [Vilyuy riv., N. Siberia]
   – *fridolini* Davenport, 1941, Bull. Harvard Mus. Comp. Zool. 87: 256
   – *grisescens* Christoph, 1893, Deut. Ent. Zeit. [Iris] 6: 87
   – *minima* Sedykh, 1977, ? Russian publication ?
   – *mixturata* Alphéraky, 1897, in Romanoff, Mèm. Lép. 9: 326
   – *witimensis* Davenport, 1941, Bull. Harvard Mus. Comp. Zool. 87: 253
ups greysh-ochre;
uns ocelli usually absent

♂ ups   ♀ ups   ♂ ups

♂ uns   ♀ uns   ♂ uns

ssp *caeca*   ssp *caeca*   ssp sub*caeca*

Talass Mts., Alabel pass,
Kirghizia

Talass Mts., Alabel pass,
Kirghizia

Sakusaku, Lake Khuvsgul,
Mongolia

♂ ups

♂ uns

ssp *subcaeca* "*elwesi*"

Akkem riv., Altai Mts.
Siberia

♂ genitalia
ssp *tullia*

Bavaria, Germany
from Higgins (1975)

ssp *caeca* Staudinger, 1886
Coenonympha caeca Staudinger, 1886, Stett. ent. Ztg. 47: 251
Type locality: Namangan Mts. [Chatkalsky Mts., Uzbekistan]
   – *eupompus* Stauder, 1924, Int. ent. Z. 17: 152
   – *heptopotamica* Sheljuzhko, 1929, Mitt. münchn. cnt. Ges.
19: 352
   – *tshonkurtshakus* Korb, 1999, **syn. nov.**
   Coenonympha tullia tshonkurtshakus Korb, 1999, Alexanor
20: 387
   taxon *tshonkurtshakus*, described from Alexandre Mts. inside
   the distribution area of ssp *caeca,* has diagnostic characters
   commonly found within the range of variability of ssp *caeca*
ups bright ochre;
uns white marks strongly developed;
unh ocelli absent

ssp *subcaeca* Heyne, 1894
Coenonympha caeca subcaeca Heyne, 1894, in Rühl, Palaearkt.
Grossschmett. 1: 827
Type locality: S. Siberia
   – *elwesi* Davenport, 1941, Bull. Harvard Mus. Comp. Zool. 87: 249
   – *sibirica* Davenport, 1941, Bull. Harvard Mus. Comp. Zool. 87: 254
   – *subcaecata* Seitz, 1908, in Seitz, Grossschmett. Erde 1: 147
ups bright ochre;
uns white marks strongly developed;
unh small ocelli present
eupompus is a form intermediate between *caeca* and *subcaeca,* that
could be just different expressions of a clinal variation

TAXONOMIC NOTE
The subspecific rank of many of the above taxa is questionable and,
as stated by Gorbunov (2001), ther presumed ranges are unnaturally
intermixed with each other. Furthermore the tendency of *tullia* to
produce clinal forms raises additional doubts on the validity of most
of the subspecies.
Taxa *caeca,* with subspecies *subcaeca,* well characterized by the ups
bright ochre colour, is given by some authors a specific rank

RANGE
ssp *tullia*: Ireland, England, S. Scotland, Central Europe from France
to West Siberia, between the 45th and 58th parallels
ssp *davus*: England, Belgium, Holland, N. E. Germany
ssp *scotica*: Scotland north of 56°N
ssp *demophile*: N. Scandinavia, N. W. Russia, N. Siberia
ssp *bosniae*: N. W. Bosnia
ssp *chatiparae*: Caucasus
ssp *caeca*: Ili region (Kazakhstan), E. Uzbekistan, Kirghizia,
Tadjikistan
ssp *subcaeca*: Altai Mts., Sajan Mts, Baikal region, Amur, Sakhalin
(Russia, China, Mongolia)
ssp *viluiensis*: from Polar Urals to Kamchatka (Russia)

many *tullia* subspecies are found in North America

SELECTED REFERENCES
Davenport (1941), Dennis (1972), Emmet & Heath (1989),
Gorbunov (2001), Rowland-Brown (1913)

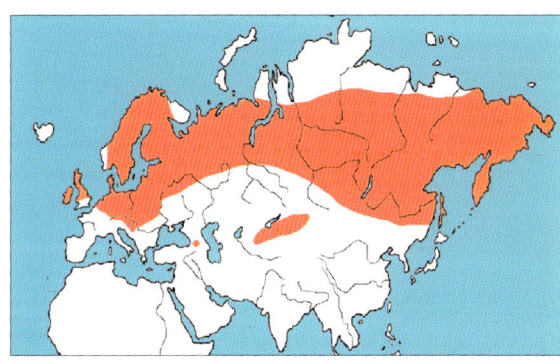

COENONYMPHA RHODOPENSIS (Elwes, 1900)

♂ ups

a

♂ uns
Mali Halan, Velebit Mts.,
Yugoslavia

♂ uns
Mali Halan, Velebit Mts.,
Yugoslavia

♀ ups

♂ uns
Mali Halan, Velebit Mts.,
Yugoslavia

♀ uns
Mali Halan, Velebit Mts.,
Yugoslavia

♂ ups

♂ uns

Monte Baldo, Trentino, Italy

♂ ups

♂ uns

Punta Meta. Marche, Italy

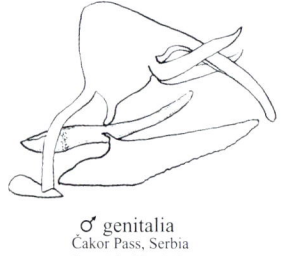

♂ genitalia
Čakor Pass, Serbia
from Jakšić (1998)

Coenonympha tiphon rhodopensis Elwes, 1900, Trans. ent. Soc. Lond. 1900: 205
Type locality: Rilo Dagh, Bulgaria
   – *italica* Verity, 1953, Farf. Diurn. Italia 5: 123
   – *molisana* Dannehl, 1933, Ent. Zeit. 46: 245
   – *occupata* Rebel, 1903, Annln naturh. Mus. Wien 18: 181
   – *tiphonides* Staudinger, 1901, in Staudinger & Rebel Catal. Lep. Pal. Fauna: 66

DIAGNOSTIC CHARACTERS
similar to *C. tullia*, but:
unf postdiscal white band absent or obsolete (a) (usually present in *C. tullia*);
unh submarginal ocelli small or absent

VARIATION
uns development of submarginal ocelli variable, ocelli small or absent in f. *occupata*

TAXONOMIC NOTE
The relationship between taxa *rhodopensis* and *tullia* is not totally clear

RANGE
Bulgaria, N. Greece, Romania, Macedonia, Montenegro, Albania, Croatia, Bosnia, N. E. Italy, C. Italy

SELECTED REFERENCES
Abadjiev (2000), Davenport (1941)

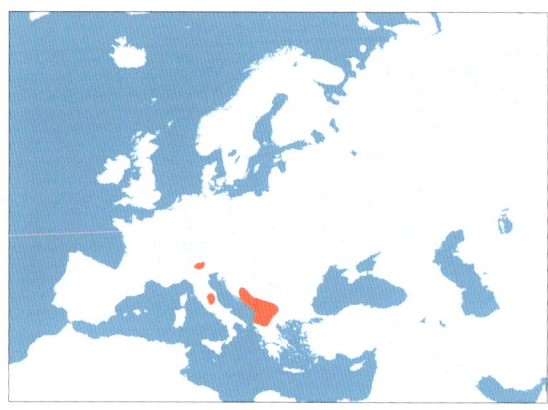

COENONYMPHA GLYCERION (Borkhausen, 1788)

σ' ups

♀ ups

σ' ups

σ' uns *ssp glycerion*
Cerknica, Lubljana,
Yugoslavia

a

σ' uns
ssp glycerion
Meiningen, Thüringen,
Germany

b

♀ uns
ssp glycerion
Meiningen, Thüringen,
Germany

σ' uns
ssp glycerion
Guzeldere Pass, Van,
E. Turkey

c

σ' uns
ssp glycerion
"*exommatica*"
Selva di Piro, Carso,
Italy

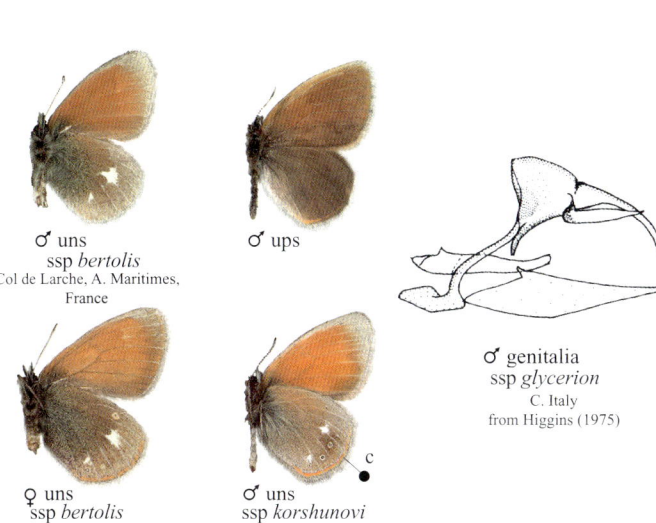

σ' uns
ssp *bertolis*
Col de Larche, A. Maritimes,
France

σ' ups

♀ uns
ssp *bertolis*
Bousson, Cesana,
Alpi Cozie, Italy

σ' uns
ssp *korshunovi*
Crimea, ai-Petri

c

σ' genitalia
ssp *glycerion*
C. Italy
from Higgins (1975)

σ' ups

σ' uns

σ' uns
HOLOTYPE

σ' uns
ssp *iphicles*
Zhang Kuang Cai Shan,
Heolonjang prov.,
Manchuria, China

♀ uns
ssp *iphicles* "*heroides*"
Yakutsk, River Lena,
Yakutia, Russia
from Dubatolov (2002)

♀ uns
ssp *iphicles* "*beljaevi*"
Primorskii Krai prov., Spassk reg.,
Novovladimirovka
from Dubatolov (2002)

Papilio glycerion Borkhausen, 1788, Naturg. eur. Schmett. 1: 90
Type locality: not stated [S. Germany]
 – *alta* Sheljutzhko, 1937, Festschr. 60: 352
 – *carpathica* Hormuzaki, 1897, Verh. zool.-bot. Ges. Wien 47: 162
 – *exommatica* Rebel, 1910, in Berge, Schmett.: 54
 – *iphis* Denis & Schiffermüller, 1775, Ank. Schmett. Wien. : 321
Extensive lists of individual forms can be found in Gaede (1931) and Verity (1953)

DIAGNOSTIC CHARACTERS
male ups ground colour brown;
male unf apical ocellus usually absent (a);

VARIATION
unh submarginal ocellation very variable: ocelli large in f. *exommatica*, ocelli small in high altitude populations;
unh shape and size of white postdiscal marks variable (b);
unh size of marginal orange-brown stripe variable (c);
unh silvery marginal line present in some populations

ssp *bertolis* de Prunner, 1798
Papilio bertolis de Prunner, 1798, Lepid. Pedemont.: 75
Type locality: Casteldelfino, Varaita valley [Maritim Alps, Italy]
 – *anaxarete* Fruhstorfer, 1910, Ent. Zeit. 24: 3
 – *belisaria* Oberthür, 1910, Etud. Lep. comp. 4: 17
unh submarginal ocelli absent or obsolete;
unh marginal area completely grey, without orange stripe

ssp *korshunovi* Nekrutenko, 1978
Coenonympha amyntas korshunovi Nekrutenko, 1978, Dopov. Akad. Nauk. Ukr. RSR 1978: 642
Type locality: Ay Petri Mt., Crimea
unh submarginal ocelli small;
unh marginal orange-brown stripe evident (c)

ssp *iphina* Staudinger, 1892
Coenonympha iphis iphina Staudinger, 1892, Deut. ent. Zeit. [Iris] 5: 339
Type locality: Tarbagatai Mts. [Kazakhstan]
ups lighter than nominal subspecies;
unh submarginal ocelli with ochre-brown rings darker than in nominal subspecies

ssp *iphicles* Staudinger, 1892
Coenonympha iphis iphicles Staudinger, 1892, Deut. ent. Zeit. [Iris] 5: 338
Type locality: Kentei Mts. [Kudara-Somon, Transbaikalia]
 – *beljaevi* Dubatolov, 1997, Far Eastern Entomologist 44: 8
 – *heroides* Christoph, 1893, Deut. ent. Zeit. [Iris] 6: 87
 – *khinganensis* Mori & Cho, 1938, Rep. Inst. scient. Res. Manchoukuo 2: 31
 – *songhioki* Im Hong An, 1988, Bull. Acad. Sci. P. R. Korea 3: 48
 – *wutaica* Murayama, 1986, Entomotaxonomia 8: 60
uph often with two or three submarginal ocelli;
unh submarginal ocelli large, with ochre-brown rings darker than in nominal subspecies

TAXONOMIC NOTE
Additional investigations would be required to ascertain the subspecific rank of the above taxa

RANGE
ssp *glycerion*: from N. Spain, through C. Europe, S. Scandinavia, Balkans, E. Turkey, Caucasus to W. Altai
ssp *bertolis*: W. Alps (Italy and France)
ssp *korshunovi*: Crimea (Ukraine)
ssp *iphina*: Saur and Tarbagatai (E. Kazakhstan)
ssp *iphicles*: from Altai, through Siberia, Mongolia, Ussuri, Amur, N. and N. E. China, N. Corea

SELECTED REFERENCES
Davenport (1941)

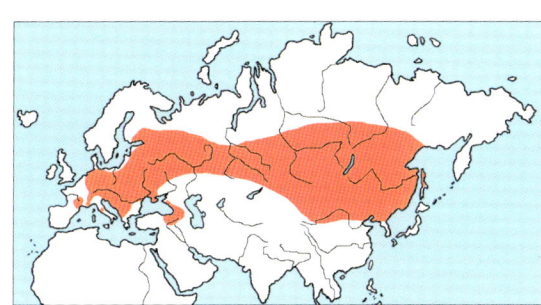

COENONYMPHA IPHIOIDES (Staudinger, 1870)

♂ ups   ♀ ups   ♂ ups

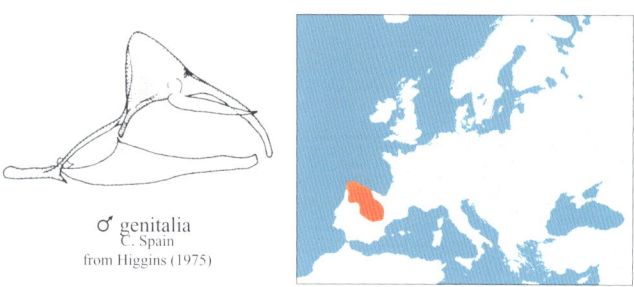

a

♂ uns   ♀ uns   ♂ uns
Abejar, Soria, Spain   Abejar, Soria, Spain   f. *pearsoni*
Porte Puymorens,
Pyrenees Orient., France

Coenonympha iphis iphioides Staudinger, 1870, Berl. ent. Z. 14: 101
Type locality: St. Ildefonso, Castilla, Spain
　　– *escudensis* Gomez-Bustillo, 1974, Revta Lep. SHILAP 1: 148
　　– *farriolsi* Marten, 1956, Ent. Zeit. 66: 185
　　– *pearsoni* Romei, 1927, Ent. Rec. 39: 137
　　– *trevincae* Wyatt, 1952, Z. wien. ent. Ges. 37: 204

DIAGNOSTIC CHARACTERS
unh ground colour orange-brown;
unh submarginal ocelli very large;
unh marginal orange-brown stripe prominent (a);
unh silvery marginal line well developed

VARIATION
form *pearsoni* Romei, 1927
Coenonympha iphioides pearsoni Romei, 1927, Ent. Rec. 39: 137
Type locality: Sierra Alta above Orihuela del Tremedal, Aragon, Spain
　　– *gallica* Ruetimeyer, 1948, Revue fr. Lép. 11: 251
　　– *pseudoamyntas* de Sagarra, 1930, Butll. Inst. Catal. Hist. nat. 10: 113
characters intermediate between *glycerion* and *iphioides*:
unh submarginal ocelli larger than in *glycerion* with yellow rings thinner than in *iphioides*;
unh white postdiscal marks small or obsolete

TAXONOMIC NOTE
The status of taxon *iphioides* is a controversial issue. Some authors rank it as subspecies of *C. glycerion*, because of the existence in E. Spain and S.W. France of populations, taxon *pearsoni*, with characters intermediate between *glycerion* and *iphioides*.
The arrangement adopted here follows the thesis that *pearsoni* is of an ancient hybrid origin. Similar cases of hybridization have been found in the same area between *Melanargia galathea* and *M. lachesis* and between *Iphiclides podalirius* and *I. feisthamelii*

RANGE
C. and N. E. Spain

SELECTED REFERENCES
Davenport (1941)

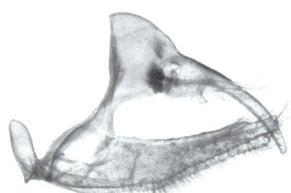

♂ genitalia
C. Spain
from Higgins (1975)

COENONYMPHA MAHOMETANA (Alphéraky, 1888)

♂ ups   ♂ ups   ♀ ups

a

♂ uns   ♂ uns   ♀ uns
Karakol, Terskey,   Teplokluchenka,   Chon Aksu riv., Kungei
Kirghizia   Kirghizia   Alatau, Kirghizia

Coenonympha iphis mahometana Alphéraky, 1881, Horae Soc. ent. ross. 16: 428
Type locality: Kounguesse [Kunes He valley, Xinjiang, N. W. China]
　　– *acelae* Hanus, 1996 **syn. nov.**
　　Coenonympha mahometana acelae Hanus, 1996, Atalanta 27: 208
　　taxon *acelae*, described from Dolon Pass in Kirghizia, has diagnostic characters commonly found within the range of variability of *C. mahometana*
　　– *decolorata* Wagner, 1913, Ent. Mitt. 2: 189
　　as stated by Davenport (1941) taxon *decolorata* is probably an hybrid between *C. mahometana* and *C. sunbecca*)

DIAGNOSTIC CHARACTERS
male ups ground colour black-brown;
unf ground colour grey-brown;
unh white submarginal ocelli blind;
unh white postdiscal band formed by separate spots (a)

VARIATION
size variable;
uns white submarginal ocelli from prominent to obsolete

RANGE
Tian Shan and Alatau (Kirghizia, E. Kazakhstan, N. W. China)

SELECTED REFERENCES
Davenport (1941)

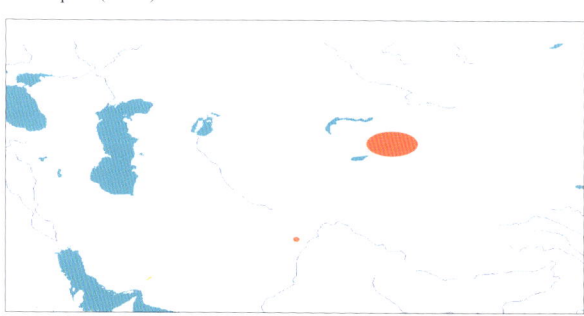

♂ genitalia
Teplokluchenka,
Kirghizia

COENONYMPHA SUNBECCA (Eversmann, 1843)

Hipparchia sunbecca Eversmann, 1843, Bull. Soc. imp. nat. Moscou 16: 538
Type locality: Noor-Saisan [Zaisan, E. Kazakhstan]
 – *alexandra* Heyne, 1894, in Rühl Pal. Grossschmett.: 624

♂ ups   ♂ ups   ♀ ups

♂ uns   ♂ uns   ♀ uns
Urumqi riv.,   Alameddin valley, N. Tian   Urumqi riv.,
Xinjiamg, China   Shan, Kirghizia   Xinjiamg, China

♂ genitalia
Urumqi riv.,
Xinjiamg, China

DIAGNOSTIC CHARACTERS
male ups ground colour light grey;
unf series of white postdiscal and submarginal blind ocelli;
unh series of white postdiscal and submarginal blind ocelli

VARIATION
size variable;
uns extension of the grey suffusion very variable, the darkest variation, more frequent in the western range, was escribed as subspecies *alexandra*

TAXONOMIC NOTE
Taxon *decolorata*: see under *C. mahometana*

RANGE
C. Asia mountains from Gissar in the west to Tarbagatai and Borohoro in the east (E. Uzbekistan, Tadjikistan, Kirghizia, E. Kazakhstan, N. W. China)

SELECTED REFERENCES
Davenport (1941)

COENONYMPHA SYMPHITA Lederer, 1870

Coenonympha symphita Lederer, 1870, Ann. Soc. ent. Belg. 13: 44
Type locality: montaigne entre Achalziche et la frontière turque [Akhaltsikhe, Georgia]
 – *karsiana* Sheljuzhko, 1929, Mitt. münchn. ent. Ges. 19: 351
 – *inocellata* Sheljuzhko, 1929, Mitt. münchn. ent. Ges. 19: 351

♂ ups   ♀ ups

♂ uns   ♀ uns
Artvin, E. Turkey   Kackar Dagi, N. Turkey

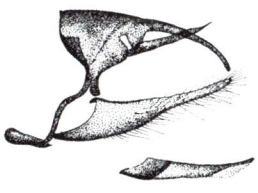

♂ genitalia
from Nekrutenko (1990)

DIAGNOSTIC CHARACTERS
unf apical ocellus present (a);
unf postdiscal light band absent;
unh regular series of small submarginal ocelli (b);
unh without postdiscal white band or white spots

VARIATION
uph 2-3 submarginal ocelli sometimes present (c);
unf size of apical ocellus variable;
unh size of submarginal ocelli variable; obsolete in f. *inocellata*

RANGE
Little Caucasus (Georgia) and N. E. Turkey

SELECTED REFERENCES
Davenport (1941), Hesselbarth et al. (1995), Nekrutenko (1990)

COENONYMPHA AMARYLLIS (Stoll, 1782)

♂ ups

♀ ups

♂ ups

♂ ups

♂ uns
ssp *amaryllis*
Narymskii Mts., S. Altai,
Bolsheriakymskol

♀ uns
ssp *amaryllis*
Balong, Burhan Budai
Shan, Qinghai, China

♂ uns
ssp *amaryllis*
Xiaojin, Qionglai Shan
Sichuan, China

♂ uns
ssp *amaryllis*
f. *accrescens*
Huaqing Spring, Qin Ling
Xian, Shaanxi, China

♂ ups

♂ ups

♂ ups

♂ ups

♂ uns
ssp *amaryllis*
50 km. E. of Batang,
W. Sichuan, China

♂ uns
ssp *amaryllis* "*borisovi*"
HOLOTYPE SZMN
Lake Baikal, Listvyanca,
S. slopes of Primorskii range,
Russia

♂ uns
ssp *pavonina*
Nanping, N. Sichuan
China

♂ uns
ssp *amaryllis*
trans. ad *tydeus*
Zhaga falls, Songpan,
N. Sichuan, China

♂ ups

♀ ups

♂ ups

♂ uns

♂ uns
ssp *tydeus*
Xinduqiao, W. Sichuan
China

♀ uns
ssp *tydeus*
Zhaga, Songpan,
N. Sichuan, China

♂ uns
ssp *tydeus* "*evanescens*"
Hongyuan, Aba conty,
N. Sichuan, China

♀ uns

Papilio amaryllis Stoll, 1782, in Cramer Uitlandsche Kapellen 4: pl. 391
Type locality: Siberia
 – *accrescens* Staudinger, 1901, in Staudinger & Rebel, Catal. Lep. Pal. Fauna: 66
 – *borisovi* Korshunov & Ivonin, 1996, in Korshunov, Additions and Corrections to the Book "Butterflies of the Asian part of Russia"
 – *leandra* Hübner, 1823, Verzeichniss bekannter Schmett. 5: 65
 – *ordossi* Alphéraky, 1889, in Romanoff, Mém. Lép. 5: 118
 – *rinda* Ménétriés, 1859, Bull. phys. math. Acad. Sci. St. Petersburg 3: 106
 – *simingica* Murayama, 1986 **syn. nov.**
Coenonympha amaryllis simingica Murayama, 1986, Entomotaxonomia 8: 60
the diagnostic characters of taxon *simingica,* from Zhejiang province in China, are within the usual variation range of nominal *amaryllis* and its form *accrescens*
 – *xinjiangensis* Chou & Huang, 1994 **syn. nov.**
Coenonympha xinjiangensis Chou & Huang, 1994, in Chou, Monographia Rhopalocerorum Sinensium, Henan
taxon *xinjiangensis* shows the diagnostic characters of *C. amarylli,* form *borisovi*; the male genitalia as well perfectly agree with those of *C. amaryllis*

DIAGNOSTIC CHARACTERS
forms with dark upperside could be confused with *C. tullia,* but the separation is usually very easy through the following characters:
uns submarginal silver line present (a), absent in *C. tullia*;
unf postdiscal dark line usually present (b), absent in *C. tullia*;
unh shape of the postdiscal white spot (c)

VARIATION
very variable:
ups ground color from ochre-yellow to brown-orange, sometimes with a dark grey margin, ocelli present or absent;
uns ocelli from large to obsolete, sometimes lacking the black circle;
unf basal and discal areas ashy grey or of the same ochre color as postdiscal and submarginal areas;
unf postdiscal dark line from very evident (b) to absent;
unh white postdiscal band from almost completely formed, to divided in spots, or reduced to a single cuneiform mark produced towards the wing base (c);
the form *accrescens* is large, has ups with ocelli evident and marginal area dusted with grey, uns with ocelli well developed; it is commonly found in the southern and eastern part of nominal *amaryllis* range and in the Baikal area, where it has been described as subspecies *borisovi*; the existence of populations intermediate between *accrescens* and nominal *amaryllis* suggests not to give the former the rank of good subspecies;
in the the north-east range the form *rinda,* with unh reduced ocelli, is frequent

ssp *pavonina* Alphéraky, 1888
Coenonympha pavonina Alphéraky, 1888, Stett. ent. Ztg. 49: 66
Type locality: Hei-po river [Nanping area, N. Sichuan, China]
ups ochreous-yellow, lighter than in nominal *amaryllis*;
ups submarginal ocelli well pronounced;
uns submarginal ocelli very large, with large white pupils

ssp *tydeus* Leech, 1892
Coenonympha typhon tydeus Leech, 1892, Butts. of China, Japan and Korea: 96
Type locality: How-kow [Xinduqiao, W. Sichuan, China]
 – *evanescens* Alphéraky, 1889 **syn. nov.**
Coenonympha amaryllis evanescens Alphéraky, 1889, in Romanoff, Mém. Lép. 5: 118
the population found in the Aba county (N. Sichuan), from where *evanescens* was described, shows the highest degree of the diagnostic characters of subspecies *tydeus*
ups dark;
unf dusted with grey;
unh submarginal ocelli small or obsolete

♂ ups   ♂ ups   ♀ ups

♂ uns
ssp *emmonsi*
Sera, W. of Lhasa, Tibet

♂ uns
ssp *forsteri*
Panga Khola, C. Nepal

♀ uns
ssp *forsteri*
Panga Khola, C. Nepal

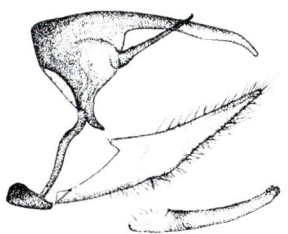

♂ genitalia
W. Altai, Bukhtarma
from Gorbunov (2001)

ssp *emmonsi* Davenport, 1941
Coenonympha amaryllis emmonsi Davenport, 1941, Bull. Harvard Mus. comp. zool. 87: 287
Type locality: Lhasa, Tibet
ups darker than ssp *tydeus*;
uns submarginall ocelli reduced to white-silvery small spots;
similar to form *evanescens* of ssp *tydeus*, but:
unf posdiscal dark line absent (often present in f. *evanescens*);
unh silvery marginal line absent (often present in f. *evanescens*)

ssp *forsteri* Gross, 1961
Coenonympha amaryllis forsteri Gross, 1961, in Forster Veroff. zool. StSamml., Munch. 6: 142
Type locality: Nepal, Mustang Heath, 29° 11' N 83° 58' E
ups as nominal *amaryllis*;
uns ocelli large, but with small black rings;
unf not dusted with grey;
unh postdiscal white spot in space 4 strongly elongated towards wing base (a);
unh two basal white stripes along cubital vein and in space 7 (b)

TAXONOMIC NOTES
The subspecific distinction between taxon *tydeus* and nominal *amaryllis* is questionable because their distribution range intermix unnaturally in N. and W. Sichuan and because of the presence of populations with intermediate characters.
In the Shaanxi region intermediate populations between *pavonina* and *amaryllis* f. *accrescens* are found as well

RANGE
ssp *amaryllis*: Asia from S. Urals to N. and E. Kazakhstan, Siberia, Mongolia, Amur, Ussuri, Central and N. W. China, Korea
ssp *pavonina*: N. Sichuan, S. Gansu (China)
ssp *tydeus*: W. Sichuan (China), S. E. Tibet
ssp *emmonsi*: C. and E. Tibet
ssp *forsteri*: Nepal

SELECTED REFERENCES
Davenport (1941)

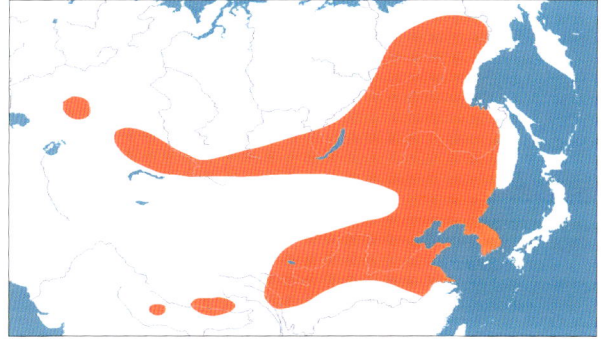

COENONYMPHA SINICA Alphéraky, 1888

Coenonympha sinica Alphéraky, 1888, Stett. ent. Ztg. 49: 64
Type locality: Steppengebiet am Fuss der Nian-Chian-Kette; Stadt Djin-ta-sy [in the dates when the type specimens were collected by Potanini, his expedition was moving to Mongolia across the Gansu stripe, north of the Qinghai lake, therefore Nian-Chian is the Qilian Shan range in N. W. Gansu, and Djin-ta-sy is probably the town of Jinta]

DIAGNOSTIC CHARACTERS
ups ground colour dark grey-brown (lighter yellow-brown in *C. amaryllis*);
uns silvery-white irregular postdiscal band (a)

TAXONOMIC NOTE
The few available specimens look very lose to *C. amaryllis*, except for the ups ground colour. Deeper investigations may bring to the conclusion that the two taxa are conspecific

RANGE
N. E. Gansu and E. Xinjiang (China). One specimen at the BMNH is labelled Ladak. The specimens quoted by Elwes (1906) from Chaksam in Tibet are not *C. sinica*, but *C. amaryllis* ssp *emmonsi*

SELECTED REFERENCES
Alphéraky (1889), Davenport (1941)

♂ uns
BMNH
Tibet H.M. Parish 1926-140

♀ ups

♀ uns
from Alphéraky (1889)

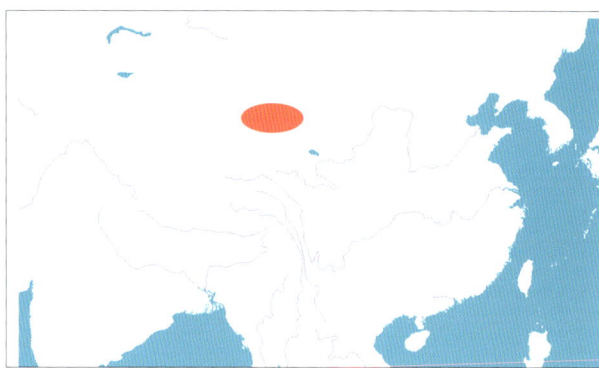

COENONYMPHA MANGERI Bang-Haas, 1927

Coenonympha mangeri Bang-Haas, 1927, Horae Macrolepidopt. 1: 50
Type locality: Pagman mont, Afghanistan [Paghman Mts.]

DIAGNOSTIC CHARACTERS
fw apical ocellus present;
unh regular series of yellow ringed submarginal ocelli;
unh yellow-white irregular postdiscal band (a)

RANGE
Paghman and Koh-i-Baba Mts., Afghanistan

SELECTED REFERENCES
Davenport (1941), Sakai (1981)

♂ ups

♂ uns
Bamian, Afghanistan

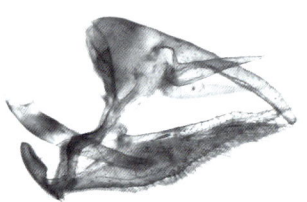

♂ genitalia
Bamian, Afghanistan

COENONYMPHA HERO (Linnaeus, 1761)

♂ ups

♀ ups

♂ uns

a

ssp *hero*
Courteney, France

♀ uns

ssp *hero*
Krakow, Dulowa, Poland

♂ ups

♀ ups

♂ ups

b

♂ uns

ssp *perseis*
Chudshirt, Changai Mts.,
Mongolia

♀ uns

ssp *perseis*
Tianchi Lake, Chang Bai
Shan, Jilin prov., China

♂ uns

ssp *latifasciata*
Makubetsu, Hokkaido,
N. Japan

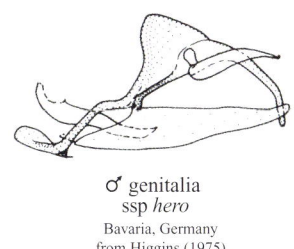

♂ genitalia
ssp *hero*
Bavaria, Germany
from Higgins (1975)

Papilio hero Linnaeus, 1761, Fauna svec.: 274
Type locality: S. Sweden
   – *sabaeus* Fabricius, 1775, Syst. Entom.: 530
   – *stolida* Schilde, 1885, Ent. Nachr. 11: 171
   An extensive list of individual forms can be found in Gaede
   (1931)

DIAGNOSTIC CHARACTERS
male ups ground colour dark grey-brown;
unh white posdiscal band;
unh metallic and an orange marginal lines (a)

VARIATION
size variable, very large specimens are found in Korea and Japan;
uph ocellation variable;
unh size of the white postdiscal band variable

ssp *perseis* Lederer, 1853
Coenonympha hero perseis Lederer, 1853, Verh. zool-bot. Ges.
Wien 5: 360
Type locality: Vorbergen des Altai zwischen Ustkamenogorsk und
Ustbuchterminsk am Irtisch [Irtysh river, W. Altai]
   – *coreana* Matsumura, 1927, Ins. Matsum. 1: 159
   – *koreuja* Seok, 1934, Bull. Kagash. Coll. 25 Anniv. 1: 677
   – *kunas* Bryk, 1942, Deut. ent. Zeit. 56: 13
   – *neoperseis* Fruhstorfer, 1908, Int. ent. Z. 2: 11
   – *pilwonis* Matsumura, 1925, Journ. Coll. Agric. Hokkaido
   imp. Univ. 15: 95
   – *sibirica* Fuchs, 1899, Jb. nass. Ver. Nat. 52: 126
uph submarginal ocelli large and bright;
unf white postdiscal band well developed (b)
unh white postdiscal band wider than in nominal *hero*

ssp *latifasciata* Matsumura, 1925
Coenonympha hero latifasciata Matsumura, 1925, Journ. Coll.
Agric. Hokkaido imp. Univ. 15: 94
Type locality: Ohtsu, Tokachi prov., Hokkaido, Japan
uns on both wings white postdiscal band very wide

TAXONOMIC NOTE
the rank of taxon *latifasciata* either as a very local subspecies
or as an individual form would require additional investigation.
Fruhstorfer described ssp *neoperseis* from Sapporo, in the
Hokkaido island, without mentioning the wide white band in
the underside

RANGE
ssp *hero*: C. Europe, S. Scandinavia, Baltic countries, Russia to
W. Siberia
ssp *perseis*: C. Asia, Mongolia, N. E. China, Korea, Japan (S.
W. Honshu)
ssp *latifasciata*: Japan (Hokkaido)

SELECTED REFERENCES
Davenport (1941)

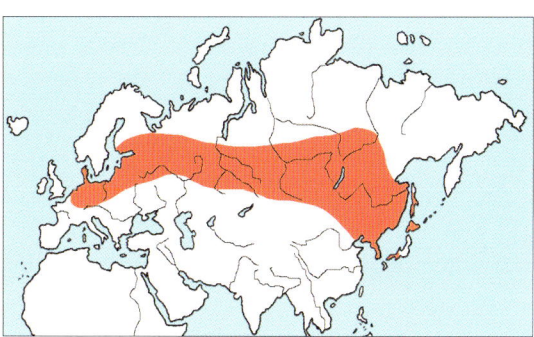

COENONYMPHA ARCANIA (Linnaeus, 1761)

♂ ups

♀ ups

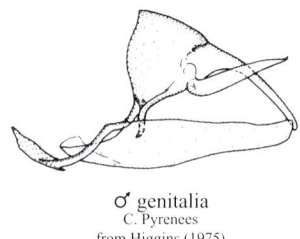

♂ uns
Valle Trebbia, Genova,
Italy

♀ uns
Valle Ponzate, Como,
Italy

●a

♂ genitalia
C. Pyrenees
from Higgins (1975)

Papilio arcania Linnaeus, 1761, Fauna svec.: 273
Type locality: Sweden
   – *amyntas* Poda, 1761, Ins. Mus. Graec.: 79
   – *caucasica* Jachontov, 1914, Revue Russe ent. 14: 298
   – *cephalus* Fourcroy, 1785, Ent. Parisiensis: 241
   – *chrysoaspida* Fruhstorfer, 1910, Ent. Zeit. 24: 4
   – *clorinda* de Sagarra, 1924, Butll. Inst. Catal. Hist. Nat. 4: 199
   – *huebneri*, Oberthür, Etud. Lep. comp. 4: 25
   – *insubrica* Frey, 1881, Mitt. scweiz. ent. Ges. 6: 353
   Extensive lists of individual forms can be found in Gaede (1931) and in Verity (1953)

DIAGNOSTIC CHARACTERS
upf ground colour fulvous with wide dark marginal borders;
unh postdiscal irregular white band widening in spaces 4 and 5;
unh submarginal ocelli ringed orange-yellow;
unh prominent ocellus in space 6 not entirely contained in the white band (a) (usually enclosed within the white band in *C. gardetta darwiniana*)

VARIATION
uph a large ochre patch may be present (form *huebneri*); common in Spain, from where it was described as subspecies *clorinda*

TAXONOMIC NOTE
In spite of the many investigations carried out by several authors, the taxonomic position and relationship between taxa *arcania*, *darwiniana*, *gardetta* and *orientalis* remains a controversial issue

RANGE
Europe from N. Spain to Urals, N. Turkey, Transcaucasia

SELECTED REFERENCES
Davenport (1941), Gross (1954), Lesse de (1949), Wiemers (1994), Wiemers (1998)

COENONYMPHA GARDETTA (de Prunner, 1798)

♂ ups   ♂ ups   ♀ ups

♂ uns
ssp *gardetta*
Valtornanche, Val d'Aosta,
Italy

♂ uns
ssp *gardetta*
Valtornanche, Val d'Aosta,
Italy

♀ uns
ssp *gardetta*
Monginevro, Piemonte,
Italy

♂ ups   ♀ ups   ♂ ups   ♀ ups

♂ uns
ssp *lecerfi*
Chalmazel. Loire,
France

♀ uns
ssp *lecerfi*
Chalmazel. Loire,
France

♂ uns
ssp *darwiniana*
San Domenico, Val di
Vedro, Italy

♀ uns
ssp *darwiniana*
Sant. Graglia, Biella,
Italy

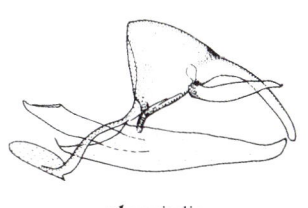

♂ genitalia
ssp *gardetta*
Switzerland
from Higgins (1975)

Papilio gardetta de Prunner, 1798, Lep. Pedemon.: 73
Type locality: valle Varaitana [Val Varaita, W. Alps, Italy]
  – *carnica* Nische, 1928, Verh. zool.-bot. Ges. Wien 78: 15
  – *chrysoaspida* Fruhstorfer, 1910, Ent. Zeit. 24: 4
  – *epiphilea* Rebel, 1910, in Berge, Schmett.-Buch: 54
  – *macrophtalmica* Galvagni, 1906, Verh. zool.-bot. Ges.
    Wien 56: 81
  – *neoclides* Hübner, 1816, Verz. bek. Schmett.: 65
  – *philea* Hübner, 1799, Schmett. Eur. 1 Pl. 53 fig. 254-255
    satyrion Esper, 1806, Schmett. Abbild. 1 Suppl.: 24
  Extensive lists of individual forms can be found in Gaede
  (1931) and in Verity (1953)

DIAGNOSTIC CHARACTERS
ssp *gardetta* and ssp *lecerfi*:
male ups almost entirely greyish;
unf apical area with a grey suffusion (a) (absent or vestigial in
C. orientalis);
unh white postdiscal band regular;
unh submarginal ocelli not ringed yellow and enclosed within
the white band

ssp *darwiniana*: see below

VARIATION
male upf size of fulvous area variable, often absent at high
altitudes;
unf small apical ocellus often present;
unh enlarged submarginal ocelli: f. *macrophtalmica*, frequent
in E. Alps

ssp *lecerfi* de Lesse, 1949
Coenonympha gardetta lecerfi de Lesse, 1949, Rev. franc. Lepid.
12: 152
Type locality: Monts du Forez, Puy-de-Dome, France
unh submarginal ocelli larger than in nominal *gardetta*;
unh marginal orange band larger than in nominal *gardetta* (b)

ssp *darwiniana* Staudinger, 1871
Coenonympha darwiniana Staudinger, 1871, Catal. Lep. Pal.
Fauna 2: 32
Type locality: Alpes Helvetia meridionalis [Valais, Switzerland]
similar to *C. arcania*, but:
unh ocellus in space 6 usually enclosed within the white band (c)
(not entirely enclosed within the white band in *C. arcania*);
unh submarginal ocelli ringed pale yellow

TAXONOMIC NOTE
See under *Coenonympha arcania*

RANGE
ssp *gardetta* : Alps (E. France, N. Italy, S. Switzerland, Austria,
S. Germany)
ssp *lecerfi*: Puy-de-Dome (France)
ssp *darwiniana*: Alps (E. France, N. Italy, S. Switzerland)

SELECTED REFERENCES
Davenport (1941), Gross (1954), Lesse de (1949), Wiemers
(1994), Wiemers (1998)

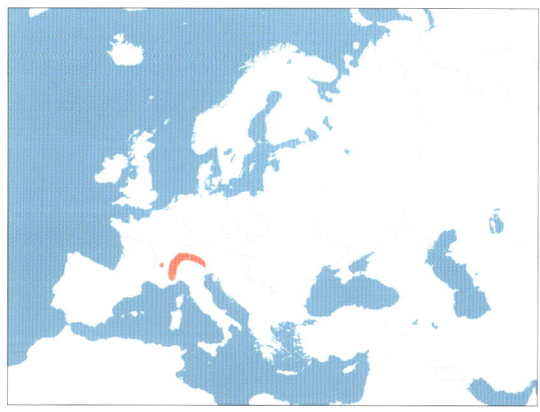

COENONYMPHA ORIENTALIS (Rebel, 1910)

a ●——

♂ ups

♀ ups

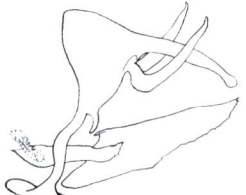

♂ uns
Katara Pass, Pindus,
Greece

♀ uns
from Tolman (1997)

♂ genitalia
Durmitor Mt., Tepca
from Jakšić (1998)

Coenonympha arcania orientalis Rebel, 1910, in Berge, Schmett.-Buch: 65
Type locality: East Bosnia
    – *katarae* Coutsis, 1972, Ent. Rec. 84: 148
    – *skypetarum* Rebel & Zerny, 1931, Denkschr. K. Akad. Wiss. Wien 103: 37

DIAGNOSTIC CHARACTERS
upf extensive fulvous discal suffusion;
uph anal angle fulvous (a);
unf apical area without grey suffusion (present in *C. gardetta*);
unh large white postdiscal band (absent in *C. leander*);
unh submarginal ocelli larger than in *C. gardetta*;
unh submarginal ocelli with yellow ring obsolete (evident in *C. leander*)

TAXONOMIC NOTE
See under *Coenonympha arcania*

RANGE
S. E. Bosnia, Montenegro, Albania and N. Greece

SELECTED REFERENCES
Boillat (1990), Davenport (1941)

COENONYMPHA ARCANIOIDES (Pierret, 1837)

♂ ups

♀ ups

♂ uns
Tikida, Djurdjura,
Algeria

♀ uns
Keddara, Alger,
Algeria

♂ genitalia
Morocco
from Higgins (1975)

Satyrus arcanioides Pierret, 1837, Annls Soc. ent. Fr. 6: 306
Type locality: Oran, Algeria
    – *holli* Oberthür, 1910, Etud. Lep. comp. 4: 20
    – *major* Seitz, 1908, Grossschmett. Erde 1: 143
    – *marginalis* Butler, 1868, Catal. Satyr. Br. Mus. p. 42

DIAGNOSTIC CHARACTERS
unh ground colour dark brown with narrow white postdiscal band

VARIATION
size variable;
unh submarginal ocelli may be reduced in size and in number

RANGE
Morocco, N. Algeria and Tunisia

SELECTED REFERENCES
Davenport (1941), Tennent (1996)

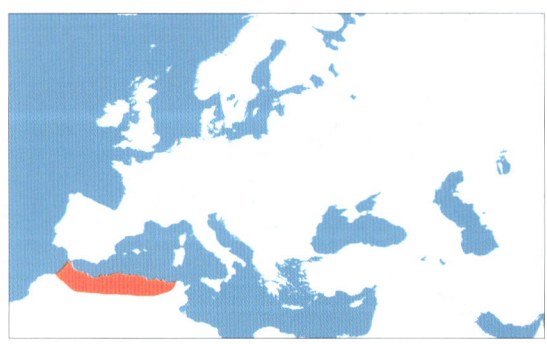

COENONYMPHA LEANDER (Esper, 1784)

♂ ups a

♂ ups

♀ ups

♂ uns b

♂ uns

♀ uns

ssp *leander*
Sarepta, Saratov, Russia

ssp *leander*
Bucovo, Ohrid, Macedonia

ssp *leander*
Sarepta, Saratov, Russia

♂ ups

ssp *leander* f. *obscura*
Toros vil., Armenia

♂ ups

♂ uns

ssp *leander* "*wageneri*"
Azerbayjan prov., E. Shand
Mt., Iran

 c

♂ ups

♀ ups

♂ ups

♂ uns
ssp *dierli*
Ala Dag, Nigde prov.,
S. Turkey

♀ uns
ssp *dierli*
Ala Dag, Nigde prov.,
S. Turkey

♂ uns
ssp *iranica*
Kondovan Tonal, Tehran
prov., Iran

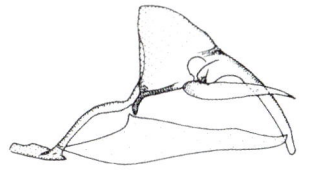

♂ genitalia
Bulgaria
from Higgins (1975)

Papilio leander Esper, 1784, Schmett. Abb. Nat. 1: 176
Type locality: an der Wolga [Volga region, Russia]
  – *clite* Hübner, 1803, Eur. Schmett. 1: 526
  – *obscura* Heyne, 1894, in Rühl. Palaearkt. Grossschmett. 1: 640
  – *philaidilis* Borkhausen, 1788, Eur. Schmett. 1: 93
  – *transcaspica* Ebert, Gross, Rose & Wagener, 1975, J. ent.
  Soc. Iran Suppl. 1: 27 **syn. nov.**
  the diagnostic characters of taxon *transcaspica*, described
  from five specimens labelled Achabad (Kopet-Dag), are the
  same commonly found in specimens from S. Russia; *C.
  leander* has never again been collected in the Kopet-Dag
  area and an erroneous labelling can not be excluded [see
  Tshikolovets, (1998)]
  – *wageneri* Ebert, Gross, Rose & Wagener, 1975, J. ent. Soc.
  Iran Suppl. 1: 26 **syn. nov.**
  the supposed diagnostic characters of taxon *wageneri*,
  described from E. Azerbaijan in Iran, are within the normal
  variation found in nominal *leander*

DIAGNOSTIC CHARACTERS
uph fulvous patch at anal angle (a);
uph black submarginal ocelli with fulvous ring;
unh white postdiscal band absent;
unh regular series of submarginal ocelli;
unh large orange band between submarginal ocelli and marginal
silvery line (b)

VARIATION
upf the basal and median fulvous flush is dark brown in form
obscura;
uph submarginal ocelli more or less evident

ssp *dierli* Koçak, 1977
Coenonympha leander dierli Koçak, 1977, Atalanta 8: 131
Type locality: Demirkazik, Aladag Mts., Turkey
male ups uniformly dark grey-brown;
female ups suffused with grey;
male unf grey

ssp *iranica* Schwingenschuss, 1939
Coenonympha leander iranica Schwingenschuss, 1939, Ent.
Zeit. 53: 86
Type locality: Elburs Mts.
male upf dark margin very narrow (c);
male uph black submarginal ocelli prominent

RANGE
ssp *leander*: E. Europe, N. Greece, Turkey, N. W. Iran, Azerbaijan,
S. Russia, Georgia, Armenia, Turkmenistan (?)
ssp *dierli*: S. Turkey
ssp *iranica*: N. Iran

SELECTED REFERENCES
Davenport (1941)

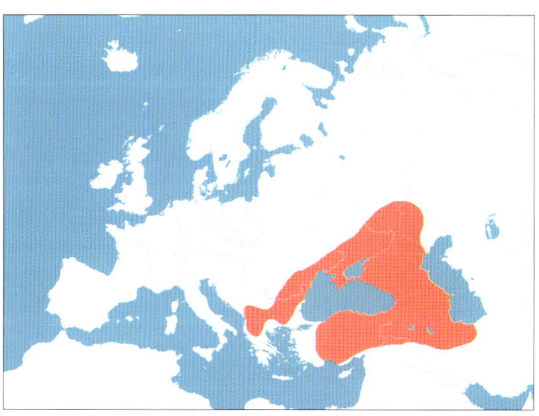

COENONYMPHA NOLCKENI Erschoff, 1874

♂ ups

♀ ups

♂ uns
Chatkalskij hr., Tian Shan,
Uzbekistan

♀ uns
Chatkalskij hr., Tian Shan,
Uzbekistan

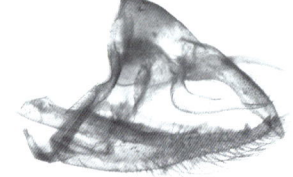

♂ genitalia
Chatkalskij hr., Tian Shan,
Uzbekistan

Coenonympha nolckeni Erschoff, 1874, Lepidoptera in
Fedtschenko Reise in Turkestan 2: 23
Type locality: monte Naubid in Turkestano Rossico
[Naubid Mt., Zeravshan, Tadjikistan]

DIAGNOSTIC CHARACTERS
large;
upf red;
uph dark grey

RANGE
Central Asia mountains from Gissar to N. Pamir, Alai and
W. Tian Shan (Uzbekistan, Tadjikistan, Kirghizia)

SELECTED REFERENCES
Davenport (1941)

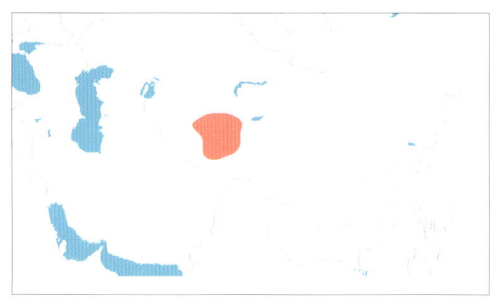

COENONYMPHA MONGOLICA Alphéraky, 1881

♂ ups

♀ ups

♂ uns

♀ uns

Tcharyn riv., Kazakhstan

Aidarly, Ili riv., Kazakhstan

♂ genitalia
Tcharyn riv., Kazakhstan

Coenonympha mongolica Alphéraky, 1881, Horae Soc.
ent. ross. 16: 426
Type locality: Kouldja [Yining (Gulja), Xinjiang, N. W.
China]

DIAGNOSTIC CHARACTERS
size larger than any other *Coenonympha* species;
ups and uns ground colour silver-grey

VARIATION
hw number of submarginal ocelli variable

RANGE
Ili, Tcharyn and Tekes valleys (E. Kazakhstan, N. W.
China)

SELECTED REFERENCES
Davenport (1941)

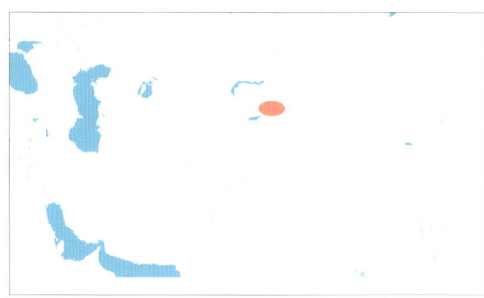

COENONYMPHA DORUS (Esper, 1782)

♂ ups

♀ ups

♂ uns · b
ssp *dorus*
St. Crepin, Briancon,
France

♀ uns
ssp *dorus*
St. Crepin, Briancon,
Franceia

♂ ups

♂ ups

♂ ups

♂ ups
Boal Carrugeiro,
Asturies, Spain
picture J. Verhulst

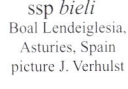

♂ uns
ssp *dorus* "*cantabrica*"
Canga de Onis, Seguenco,
Asturies, Spain

♂ uns
ssp *dorus* "*fonti*"
Noguera, Aragon,
Spain

♂ uns
ssp *dorus* "*andalusica*"
Puerto de Zegri, Granada,
Spain

♂ uns
ssp *bieli*
Boal Lendeiglesia,
Asturies, Spain
picture J. Verhulst

♂ ups

♀ ups

a

♂ uns
ssp *dorus* "*aquilonia*"
Prunarolo, App. Tosco-
Emiliano, Italy

♀ uns
ssp *dorus* "*aquilonia*"
Prunarolo, App. Tosco-
Emiliano, Italy

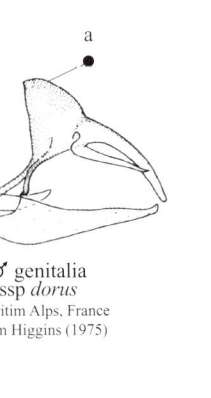

♂ genitalia
ssp *dorus*
Maritim Alps, France
from Higgins (1975)

Papilio dorus Esper, 1782, Schmett. 1: 130
Type locality: Languedoc [S. France]
- – *aquilonia* Higgins, 1969, Entomologist 102: 60
- – *andalusica* Ribbe, 1906, Deut. Ent. Zeit. [Iris] 19: 243
- – *cantabrica* Agenjo, 1953, Graellsia 11: 1
- – *dorilis* Borkhausen, 1788, Nat. Europ. Schmett.: 93
- – *dorion* Hübner, 1799, Ges. Europ. Schmett. pl. 52 f. 247-248
- – *fonti* de Sagarra, 1924, Butll. Inst. catal. Hist. nat. 4: 199
- – *lisetta* Cramer, 1782, Papillons exot. 4: 166
- – *microphtalma* Oberthür, 1910, Etud. Lep. comp. 4: 33
- – *purpurinatta* Gomez Buztillo, 1973, Revta Lep. SHILAP 1: 26
Extensive list of *dorus* synonyms and forms can be found in Gaede (1931) and Verity (1953)

DIAGNOSTIC CHARACTERS
male genitalia: tegumen steeply domed (a);
hw ocellus in space 6 displaced distally (b)

VARIATION
very variable in the following characters:
size;
uph extension of the dark suffusion;
hw number of submarginal ocelli;
uns ground colour ranging from yellow to grey-brown

among the subspecies described from Spain, *cantabrica* from N. Spain, with uph heavily suffused with brown and unh ocelli large and *andalusica* from S. Spain, with unh ground colour pale and ocelli small, seem questionable because populations with intermediate characters are commonly found; a deeper investigation would be required to ascertain their subspecific rank; here only the following subspecies are retained:

ssp *bieli* Staudinger, 1901
Coenonympha dorus bieli Staudinger, 1901, in Staudinger & Rebel Catal. Lep. Pal. Fauna: 65
Type locality: Oporto, Villa Real, Portugal
- – *mathewi* Tutt, 1904, Ent. Rec. 16: 308
- – *semibieli* Verity, 1929, Bull. Soc. ent. Fr.: 185
male uph suffused with brown or with a small orange patch;
both wings ocelli small;
uns ground colour orange-brown;

ssp *cerratoi* Rojio, 1997
Coenonympha dorus cerratoi Rojio, 1997, Boletin de la SEA 18: 66
Type locality: Astudillo, Palencia, Spain
both wings ocelli absent or vestigial;
upf totally obscured

TAXONOMIC NOTE
For the relationship between taxa *dorus*, *fettigii* and *austauti* see under *C. fettigii*

RANGE
ssp *dorus*: S. France, Spain, W. and C. Italy
ssp *bieli*: N. Spain, C. and N. Portugal
ssp *cerratoi*: N. Spain, known only from the type locality

SELECTED REFERENCES
Boillat (1989), Gomez Bustillo & Fernandez-Rubio (1974), Davenport (1941)

COENONYMPHA FETTIGII Oberthür, 1874

♂ ups   ♂ ups   ♀ ups

♂ uns   ♂ uns   ♀ uns
ssp *fettigii* ssp *fettigii* ssp *fettigii*
Sebdou, Algeria Tizi n Test, High Atlas, Tizi n Test, High Atlas,
     Morocco   Morocco

♂ ups

♂ genitalia
ssp *fettigii*
High Atlas, Morocco
from Higgins (1975)

♂ uns
ssp *nicholasi*
Glaciere de Blida, Algeria
from Oberthür (1910)

Coenonympha fettigii Oberthür, 1874, Petites Nouv. ent. 1: 412
Type locality: Telaghre, Algeria
 – *inframaculata* Oberthür, 1922, Etud. Lep. comp. 19: 87

DIAGNOSTIC CHARACTERS
similar to *C. dorus*, but:
upf with a large orange postdiscal band broken by veins (a);
upf apical ocellus usually small;
uph submarginal ocelli absent or small;
unh ground colour yellowish-grey;
unh submarginal ocelli small or absent

VARIATION
very variable:
upf orange suffusion often reduced;
unh size of the postdiscal light band from small to very large: the
form with a large band was described from Morocco as subspecies
inframaculata, but the variability of this character in Moroccan
populations does not support a subspecific rank for this taxon;
uns ocellation variable

ssp *nicholasi* Rothschild, 1925
Coenonympha dorus nicholasi Rothschild, 1925, Novit. zool. 32: 208
Type locality: Glacierse de Blida, Algeria
 – *holli* Oberthür, 1910, Etud. Lep. comp. 4: 42
upf orange suffusion more extensive than in nominal *fettigii*

TAXONOMIC NOTE
The relationship between taxa *dorus*, *fettigi* and *austauti* is not totally
clear and deeper investigations may bring changes to the current
taxonomic arrangement

RANGE
ssp *fettigii*: Morocco, W. Algeria
ssp *nicholasi*: E. Algeria, Tunisia

SELECTED REFERENCES
Boillat (1989), Davenport (1941), Tennent (1996)

COENONYMPHA AUSTAUTI (Oberthür, 1881)

♂ ups   ♀ ups

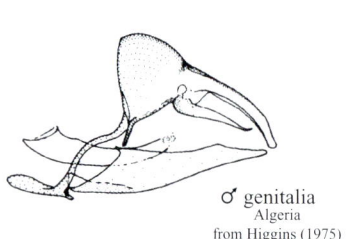

♂ uns   ♀ uns
Nedroma, Orano, Algeria Nedroma, Orano, Algeria

♂ genitalia
Algeria
from Higgins (1975)

Coenonympha dorus austauti Oberthür, 1881, Etud. ent. 6: 59
Type locality: Nemours [Ghazaouet, Algeria]

DIAGNOSTIC CHARACTERS
upf with a large orange postdiscal band broken by veins, as in *C.
fettigii* (a);
upf apical ocellus large (b);
uph usually with blind submarginal ocelli (c);
unh ground colour yellowish-grey;
unh white postdiscal band narrow, but prominent;
unh submarginal ocelli large;
unh marginal silver line larger than in *C. dorus* (d)

VARIATION
upf orange suffusion variable

TAXONOMIC NOTE
See under *C. fettigii*

RANGE
W. Algeria, N. E. Morocco

SELECTED REFERENCES
Boillat (1989), Davenport (1941), Tennent (1996)

COENONYMPHA VAUCHERI Blachier, 1905

♂ ups   ♀ ups

♂ uns   ♀ uns
ssp *vaucheri*   ssp *vaucheri*
Imlil, H. Atlas, Morocco   Imlil, H. Atlas, Morocco

♂ ups   ♀ ups   ♂ ups
                                    ● a

♂ uns   ♀ uns   ♂ uns
                                    ● a
ssp *annoceuri*   ssp *annoceuri*   ssp *beraberensis*
Taghzeft, M. Atlas, Taghzeft, M. Atlas, Dj. Aourach, Morocco
Morocco   Morocco   from Tennent (1996)

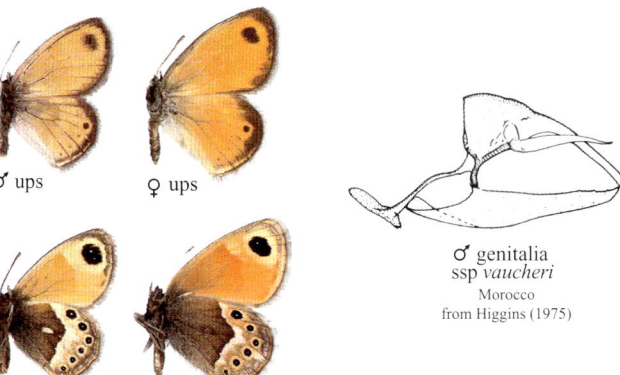

♂ ups   ♀ ups

♂ uns   ♀ uns
ssp *rifensis*   ssp *rifensis*
Dj. Lakra, W.   Dj. Lakra, W.
Chechaoun, Rif,   Chechaoun, Rif,
Morocco   Morocco

♂ genitalia
ssp *vaucheri*
Morocco
from Higgins (1975)

Coenonympha vaucheri Blachier, 1905, Bull. Soc. ent. Fr. 1905: 213
Type locality: High Atlas Mts., Morocco

DIAGNOSTIC CHARACTERS
unh basal area dark with a pale mark in the cell

VARIATION
markings and ocellation variable

ssp *annoceuri* Wyatt, 1952
Coenonympha vaucheri annoceuri Wyatt, 1952, Z. wien. ent.
Ges. 37: 175
Type locality: Annoceur, Morocco
both wings ocelli smaller than in nominal *vaucheri*;
ups usually without dark suffusion

ssp *rifensis* Weiss, 1979
Coenonympha vaucheri rifensis Weiss, 1979, Entomops 48: 271
Type locality: Chaouen, Morocco
ups pale orange;
both wings ocelli small;
unh submarginal ocelli encircled by yellow

ssp *beraberensis* Lay & Rose, 1979
Coenonympha vaucheri beraberensis Lay & Rose, 1979, Ent.
Zeit. 89: 143
Type locality: Tizi-n' Ouguerd-Zegzaoune, Morocco
both wings ocelli very large;
fw outer third pale yellow (a)

RANGE
ssp *vaucheri*: Morocco (High Atlas)
ssp *annoceuri*: Morocco (Middle Atlas)
ssp *rifensis*: Morocco (W. Rif Mts.)
ssp *beraberensis*: Morocco (High Atlas)

SELECTED REFERENCES
Davenport (1941), Tennent (1996)

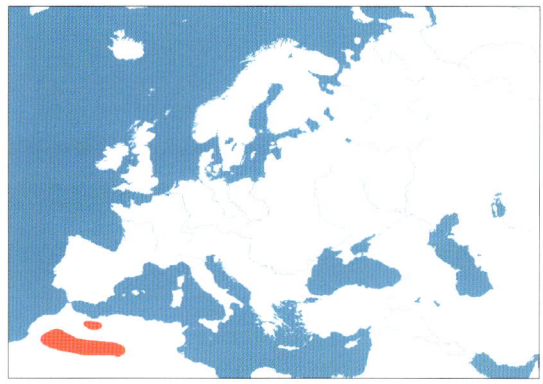

COENONYMPHA CORINNA (Hübner, 1803)

Papilio corinna Hübner, 1803, Europ. Schmett. f. 536-537
Type locality: Sicily [probably a mistake, since there has not been
any subsequent record of *C. corinna* from Sicily]
— *corinus* Godart, 1823, Encyc. Meth. 9: 547
— *norax* Bonelli, 1826, Mem. R. Accad. Sci. Torino 30: 183
Extensive lists of individual forms can be found in Gaede
(1931) and Verity (1953)

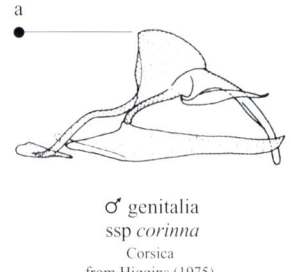

ssp *corinna*
Monte Spada, Sardinia,
Italy

ssp *trettaui*
Capraia Is., Italy

DIAGNOSTIC CHARACTERS
male genitalia: tegumen domed (a) (scarcely domed in *C. elbana*);
unh grey basal area defined by a yellowish irregular postdiscal band (b);
unh submarginal ocelli in space 2, 3 and 4, if present, small and in a straight row

VARIATION
ocellation variable

ssp *trettaui* Gross, 1970
Coenonympha corinna trettaui Gross, 1970, Ent. Zeit. 80: 161
Type locality: Capraia Is.
unh ocelli more developed than in nominal *corinna*;
unh one or two basal white spots are present (c)

TAXONOMIC NOTE
Recent researchs using enzyme electrophoresis have confirmed the rank of good species for taxa *corinna* and *elbana* and the status of subspecies of *C. corinna* for taxon *trettaui* (Sbordoni in litteris 2002)

RANGE
ssp *corinna*: Sardinia (Italy) and Corsica (France)
ssp *trettaui*: Capraia Is. (Italy)

SELECTED REFERENCES
Davenport (1941), Jutzeler & de Bros (1996); Jutzeler & de Bros (1997)

♂ genitalia
ssp *corinna*
Corsica
from Higgins (1975)

COENONYMPHA ELBANA (Staudinger, 1901)

Coenonympha corinna elbana Staudinger, 1901, in Staudinger & Rebel, Catal. Lep. Pal. Fauna 1: 66
Type locality: Elba, Italy
— *altera* Verity, 1917, Boll. Soc. ent. ital. 48: 192
— *lefebvrei* Ragusa, 1908, Naturalista sicil. 30: 140

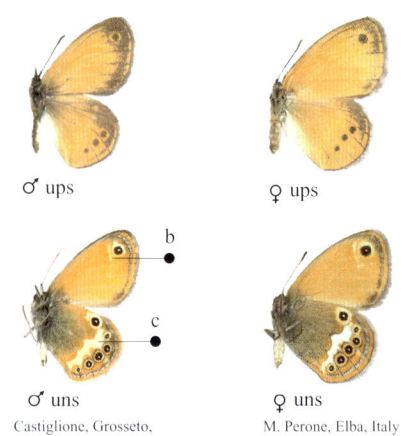

σ ups

♀ ups

σ uns
Castiglione, Grosseto,
Italy

♀ uns
M. Perone, Elba, Italy

DIAGNOSTIC CHARACTERS
male genitalia: tegumen scarcely domed (a) (domed in *C. corinna*);
uns black submarginal and marginal lines equally well developed (only marginal line evident in *C. corinna*);
male unf with a light band close to apical ocellus (absent in *C. corinna*) (b);
uph submarginal ocelli well developed;
unh submarginal ocelli well developed;
unh yellowish postdiscal band more regular than in *C. corinna* (c)

TAXONOMIC NOTE
See under *C. corinna*

RANGE
Elba and nearby islands, Tuscany coast (Italy)

SELECTED REFERENCES
Davenport (1941); Jutzeler, Biermann & de Bros (1996)

♂ genitalia
Elba
from Higgins (1975)

COENONYMPHA SAADI (Kollar, 1850)

♂ ups   ♀ ups   ♂ ups   ♀ ups

♂ uns   ♀ uns   ♂ uns   ♀ uns
ssp *saadi*   ssp *saadi*   ssp *saadi*   ssp *saadi*
Dasht-e-Arzan,   Gachsar, Tehran, Iran   South Zangezur Mts.,   South Zangezur Mts.,
Shiraz, Iran   Transcaucasus, Armenia   Transcaucasus, Armenia

♂ ups   ♂ ups   ♀ ups

♂ uns   ♂ uns   ♀ uns
ssp   ssp   ssp
mesopotamica   *mesopotamica*   *mesopotamica*
Birecik, Gaziantep,   Narince, Adiyaman,   Halfeti, Gaziantep,
Turkey   Turkey   Turkey

♂ genitalia
ssp *saadi*
from Nekrutenko (1990)

Satyrus saadi Kollar, 1850, Denkschr. K. Akad. Wiss. Wien 1: 52
Type locality: S. Iran [Fars, Iran]
    – *iphias* Eversmann, 1851, Bull. Soc. imp. Nat. Moscou 24: 618

DIAGNOSTIC CHARACTERS
unf one or two large black spots in space 3 and 4 (a);
unf black postdiscal line distally bordered white (b)

VARIATION
upf ocellus in space 3 often absent in Turkish populations

ssp *mesopotamica* Heyne, 1894
Coenonympha saadi mesopotamica Heyne, 1894, in Rühl, Pal.
Grossschmett. 1: 617
Type locality: Mesopotamia [S. E. Turkey]
fw ocellus in space 3 usually absent;
uns yellow-grey, lighter than nominal *saadi*, with reduced
markings

TAXONOMIC NOTE
Populations from E. Turkey are intermediate between ssp
mesopotamica and nominal *saadi*.
The populations from Transcaucasia have been included by some
authors in ssp *mesopotamica*, but they don't seem to show any
significant difference from nominal *saadi*

RANGE
ssp *saadi*: C. and N. Iran, Iraq, Transcaucasia
ssp *mesopotamica*: S. E. Turkey

SELECTED REFERENCES
Davenport (1941)

COENONYMPHA THYRSIS (Freyer, 1845)

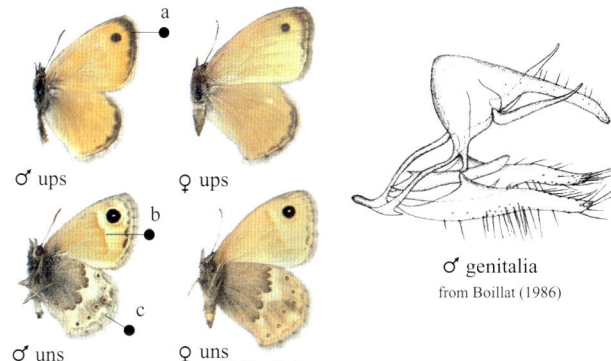

♂ ups   ♀ ups

♂ uns   ♀ uns
M. Ida, Crete   M. Ida, Crete

♂ genitalia
from Boillat (1986)

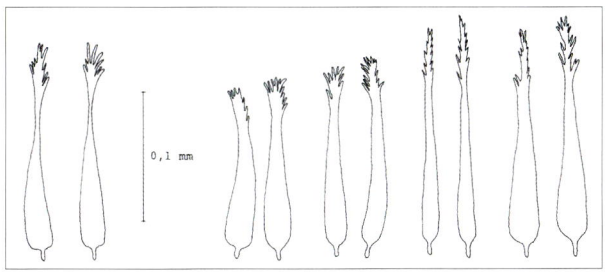

0,1 mm

C. thyrsis   *C. pamphilus lyllus*
♂ androconial scales
from Boillat (1986)

Hipparchia thyrsis Freyer, 1845, Neuere Beitr. 5 pl. 475 fig. 1
Type locality: Crete Island
    – *cretica* Stanfuss, 1855, Stett. ent. Ztg. 16: 158

DIAGNOSTIC CHARACTERS
male genitalia uncus, falces and aedeagus shorter than in *C.
pamphilus*;
androconial scales with shape different from *C. pamphilus*;
ups dark marginal border conspicuous (a);
unf dark postdiscal line well defined (b);
unh submarginal ocelli followed distally by a silvery line (c)

RANGE
Crete Island (Greece)

SELECTED REFERENCES
Boillat (1986), Davenport (1941)

COENONYMPHA PAMPHILUS (Linnaeus, 1758)

♂ ups   ♀ ups   ♂ ups

♂ uns
Novi di Modena,
Italy

♀ uns
Val Ponzate, Como,
Italy

♂ uns
f. *marginata*
M. Parnis, Athens,
Greece

♂ ups   ♀ ups

♂ uns
f. *lyllus*
Ifrane, M. Atlas,
Morocco

♀ uns
f. *lyllus*
Cistierna, Leon,
Spainy

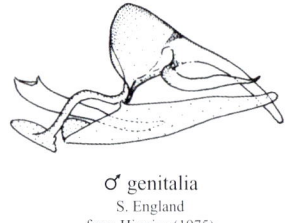

♂ genitalia
S. England
from Higgins (1975)

Papilio pamphilus Linnaeus, 1758, Syst. Natur. ed. 10: 472
Type locality: not stated [Sweden]
    – *australis* Verity, 1914, Boll. Soc. ent. ital. 45: 227
    – *lyllus* Esper, 1805, Schmett. Abbild. Suppl. 2: 23
    – *marginata* Heyne, 1894, in Rühl, Pal. Grossschmett. 1: 619
    – *rhoumensis* Harrison, 1948, Ent. Rec. 60: 111
    – *scota* Verity, 1910, Boll. Soc. ent. ital. 42: 271
    – *semilyllus* Krulikowsky, 1908, Soc. ent. 23: 3
    Extensive lists of forms and synonyms can be found in Gaede (1931) and Verity (1953)

DIAGNOSTIC CHARACTERS
ups grey marginal border 1-2 mm wide (a)

VARIATION
very variable individually, locally and through seasons:
ups ground colour variable;
ups width of dark marginal border variable, very broad in f. *marginata,* common in summer broods particularly, but not only, in Greece and Turkey;
unf additional ocelli sometimes present;
unf a pale postdiscal line sometimes present (b);
unh development of the pale patch bordering the dark basal area variable from extended across the wing to obsolete;
unh ground colour variable from light grey to brown;
unh submarginal ocelli sometimes obsolete

f. *lyllus,* usual in summer broods in all the southern range of *C. pamphilus*, shows in unf a well defined postdiscal transverse line (c) and has unh pale sandy-brown with markings brown, often indistinct

TAXONOMIC NOTE
As stated by Tennent (1996) taxon *lyllus* has been referred to by different authors as species, subspecies, seasonal or geographical form. Its characters are evident only in summer broods, while early and late broods resemble typical *pamphilus*

RANGE
Europe, N. Africa, Turkey, Iraq, Iran, Caucasus, Russia to W. Siberia

SELECTED REFERENCES
Davenport (1941), Verity (1926)

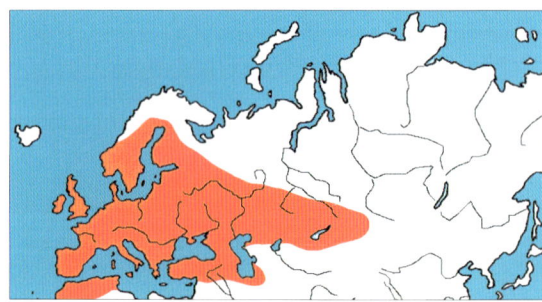

COENONYMPHA SEMENOVI Alphéraky, 1887

♂ ups   ♀ ups   ♂ ups

♂ uns
ssp *semenovi*
Balong, Burhan
Budai Shan,
Qinghai, China

♀ uns
ssp *semenovi*
Balong, Burhan
Budai Shan,
Qinghai, China

♂ uns
ssp *semenovi* "*arnoldi*"
Xihae, Gansu, China

♂ ups   ♂ ups   ♂ ups

  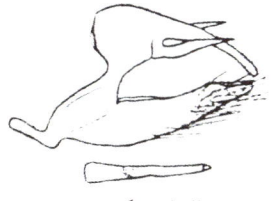

♂ uns
ssp *leanotchka*
Mugeco Lake, Kangding,
Sichuan, China

♂ uns
ssp *sala*
PARATYPE
Heimahe, Kukunor,
Qinghai, China

♂ uns
ssp *?*
Barkham, Qionglai Shan,
Sichuan, China

♂ uns
ssp *jiadengyuica*
HOLOTYPE
from Huang &
Murayama (1992)

♂ genitalia
from Davenport (1941)

Coenonympha semenovi Alphéraky, 1887, in Romanoff 3: 405
Type locality: de la chaine Bourkhane-Bouddha (Tsaidame)
[Burhan Budai Shan, Qinghai, China]
   – *arnoldi* Bang-Haas, 1934, Ent. Zeit. 48: 110
   – *vera* Kocman, 1996, **syn. nov.**
   Coenonympha semenovi vera Kocman, 1996, Lambillionea
96: 41

   taxon *vera* from N. Qinghai does not show any character
differing from nominal *semenovi*; its author probably has
been mislead having compared this taxon with the dark, and
very common, ssp *leanotchka*, rather than with the true, and
less common, nominal *semenovi*

DIAGNOSTIC CHARACTERS
uph series of white submarginal spots

VARIATION
very variable;
f. *arnoldi*, with ups ground colour rich brown, is constant in the
eastern part of the range, and it is linked to the nominal form by
populations with transition characters;
unf white postdiscal spots often present;

ssp *leanotchka* Hemming, 1933
Coenonympha semenovi leanotchka Hemming, 1933,
Entomologist 66: 275
Type locality: Tatsienlu [Kangding, Sichuan, China]
   – *obscura* Alphéraky, 1897, in Romanoff 9: 111
   – *szechwana* Bang-Haas, 1934, Ent. Zeit. 48: 110
ups dull grey-brown

ssp *jiadengyuica* Huang & Murayama, 1992
Coenonympha semenovi jiadengyuica Huang & Murayama,
1992, Tyo to Ga 43: 5
Type locality: Jiadengyu, Altai, Xinjiang prov., China
ups without white markings;
unf a postdiscal black edged white band

ssp *sala* Kocman, 1995
Coenonympha semenovi sala Kocman, 1996, Lambillionea 95: 67
Type locality: road Chaka - Wulan, Qinghai, China
both sides ground colour lighter than nominal *semenovi*

TAXONOMIC NOTE
C. semenovi seems to have a tendency to randomly produce
populations with very light ground colour; the author has found
a population as light as ssp *sala*, but with a colder grey, well
inside the range of ssp *leanotchka*. Subspecies *sala* as well is
found inside the range of nominal *semenovi*. The rank of these
light forms is questionable.
More material would be required to ascertain the status of ssp
jiadengyuica

RANGE
ssp *semenovi*: Qinghai
ssp *leanotchka*: W. Sichuan
ssp *jiadengyuica*: Altai (N. Xinjiang, China) only the type series,
one male and two females, seem to be known
ssp *sala*: N. Qinghai (China)

SELECTED REFERENCES
Davenport (1941)

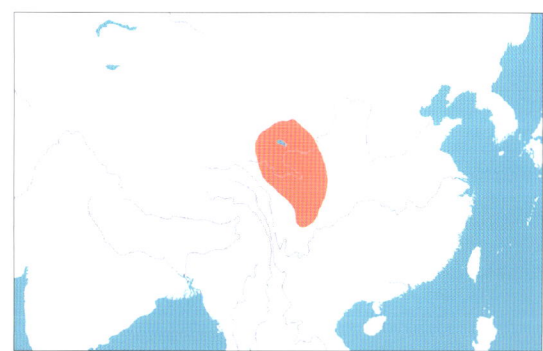

COENONYMPHA OEDIPPUS (Fabricius, 1787)

♂ ups

♀ ups

♂ uns — a
Vittorio V., Treviso,
Italy

♀ uns — b
Vittorio V., Treviso,
Italy

♂ uns
oedippus "mariae"
Cameri, Ticino riv.,
Italy

♂ uns — d

oedippus "magna"
Chang Bai Shan,
Jilin prov., China

♂ uns

oedippus "tabaica"
Huaqing Springs, Qin
Ling, Shaanxi, China

♂ uns — c
oedippus "annulifer"
Ishigure, Honshu, Japan

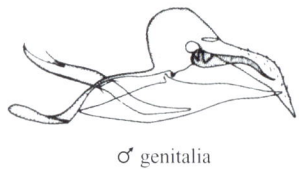

♂ uns
oedippus "annulifer"
Sinano-Oiwaka, Nagano, Japan
picture S. Sakai

♂ uns
oedippus "arothius"
Nishinomiya, Japan
picture S. Sakai

♂ genitalia
S. E. France
from Higgins (1975)

Papilio oedippus Fabricius, 1787, Mantissa Insect. 2: 31
Type locality: in Russia australiori [S. Russia]
– *amurensis* Heyne, 1895, in Rühl, Palaearkt. Grossschmett.: 607
– *annulifer* Butler, 1877, Ann. Mag. nat. Hist. 19: 91
– *arothius* Okada & Torii, 1945, Trans. Nip. Lep. Soc. 1: 4
– *geticus* Esper, 1790, Schmett. pl. 102 f. 2
– *herbuloti* Varin, 1952, Lambillionea 52: 5
– *hungarica* Aigner,1910, in Berge Schmett. Buch.: 53
– *magna* Heyne, 1895, in Rühl, Palaearkt. Grossschmett.: 608
– *mariae* Rocci, 1928, Boll. Soc. ent. It. 60: 51
– *monticola* Kolar, 1922, Verh. zool.-bot. Ges. Wien 71: 12
– *pedemontana* Rocci, 1928, Boll. Soc. ent. It. 60: 51
– *rhenana* Gradl, 1933, Int. ent. Z. 27: 257
– *sebrica* Varin, 1952, Lambillionea 52: 5
– *steni* Bryk, 1946, Arkiv zool. 38A: 23
– *tabaica* Murayama, 1986, Entomotaxonomia 8: 60

Extensive lists of individual forms and synonyms can be found in Davenport (1941), Gaede (1931) and Verity (1953)

DIAGNOSTIC CHARACTERS
male genitalia uncus with central expansion, brachia sinuous;
ups uniformly dark brown;
unh ocellus in space 6 displaced basally (a)

VARIATION
very variable in the follwing characters:
size;
uph submarginal ocelli from obsolete to well developed, with a white pupil;
uns ground colour from grey-brown to reddish-brown, but quite constant in single populations; in f. *monticola* from S. Tyrol ground colour dark brown;
unf number of submarginal ocelli from four to none;
unh size of ocelli; very reduced in f. *hungarica*; usually large in the eastern area of the range;
unh an additional ocellus is often present in space 5 (b);
unh a white postdiscal band may be present (c);
unh marginal metallic line from evident to obsolete (d)

all the above variations are found in the whole distribution range of *C. oedippus*, therefore the many described subspecies should not be taken into consideration

TAXONOMIC NOTE
the rank of taxa *magna* and *annulifer* is questionable because their diagnostic characters are very variable

RANGE
C. Europe, Russia, C. Asia, Amur, Ussuri, Mongolia, C. and N. E. China, Korea, Japan

SELECTED REFERENCES
Davenport (1941)

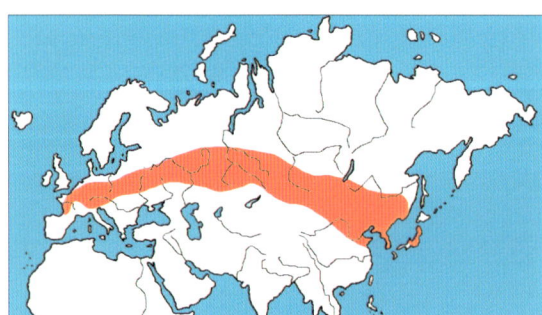

genus **TRIPHYSA** Zeller, 1850

Triphysa Zeller, 1850, Stett. ent. Ztg **11**: 311
Type species: *Papilio tircis* Stoll, 1782
    – *Phryne* Herrich-Schäffer, [1844], Syst. Bearb. Schmett. Europ. **1**: 90

DIAGNOSTIC CHARACTERS
eyes naked;
antennae very short, strongly clubbed;
palpi short;
male genitalia: tegumen domed, uncus longer than tegumen, with rounded apex, valve wide with pointed apex, apical part
of aedeagus with large lateral spines;
forewing base of veins 1, subcostal and cubital swollen

RANGE
Found only in the Palaearctic region

CHECKLIST OF THE SPECIES FOUND IN THE PALEARCTIC REGION
phryne (Pallas, 1771)
dohrnii dohrnii Zeller, 1850
    dohrnii biocellata (Staudinger, 1901)
    dohrnii gartoki (Bang-Haas, 1929)
    dohrnii glacialis (Bang-Haas, 1912)
    dohrnii nervosa (Motschulsky, 1866)

TRIPHYSA PHRYNE (Pallas, 1771)

Papilio phryne Pallas, 1771, Reise Prov. Russ. Reiches 1: 5 72
Type locality: ... Volgae versus Sysranum [Oktyabrskiy, Syzran Distr., Samara, Russia]

DIAGNOSTIC CHARACTERS
male genitalia falces very short (a) (much longer in *T. dohrnii*);
ups white marginal line well developed (b);
unh with a complete series of premarginal ocelli;
unh premarginal ocelli with white pupil

TAXONOMIC NOTE
The separation of *T. phryne* from all the related taxa is easy, even when the external characters are similar, because of the sharp and constant difference in the male genitalia

RANGE
S. Russia, E. Turkey? (no recent record and not even mentioned from Caucasus)

♂ ups

♀ ups

♂ uns
Saratov, Russia

♀ uns
Bredy, S. Ural, Russia

♂ genitalia
Kuvandyk, S. Ural
from Gorbunov (2001)

♂ genitalia
Saratov, Russia

TRIPHYSA DOHRNII Zeller, 1858

♂ ups

♀ ups

♂ ups

♂ uns
ssp *dohrnii*
Aktasch, Altai Mts.

♀ uns
ssp *dohrnii*
S.-W. Altai, border with
China and Mongolia,
Russia

♂ uns
ssp *glacialis* "*sacha*"
sacha HOLOTYPE
SZMN
Yakutia, Yakutsk,
botanical garden

♂ uns
ssp *glacialis*
Jakutsk, Siberia

♂ uns
ssp *glacialis*
Jakutsk, Siberia

♀ uns
ssp *glacialis*
Jakutsk, Siberia

♂ ups

♂ ups

♂ ups

♂ uns
ssp *nervosa*
Bilibino, Chukotka,
Far East Russia

♂ uns
ssp *biocellata*
Linxia, Gansu, China

♂ uns
ssp *gartoki*
40 km W. of Gar, W. Tibet

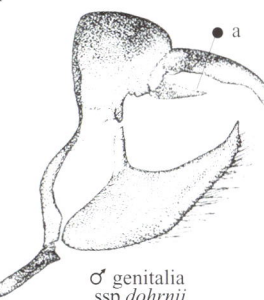

♂ genitalia
ssp *dohrnii*
Aktasch, Altai Mts.
from Gorbunov (2001)

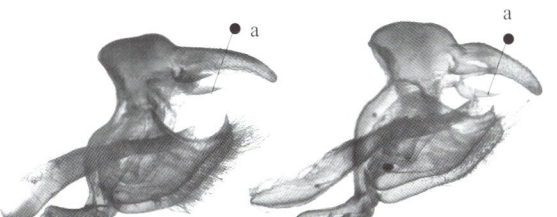

♂ genitalia
ssp *gartoki*
40 km W. of Gar, W. Tibet

♂ genitalia
ssp *biocellata*
Linxia, Gansu, China

Triphysa dohrnii Zeller, 1850, Stett. ent. Ztg. 11: 308
Type locality: ... sudlichen Russland [S. Siberia ?]
   – *tircis* Stoll, 1782, in Cramer, Pap. exot. 4: 373
   – *striatula* Elwes, 1899, Trans. ent. Soc. Lond. 1899: 365

DIAGNOSTIC CHARACTERS
male genitalia falces long (a) (very short in *T. phryne*);
uns submarginal ocelli, when present, usually without white pupil

VARIATION
ups white marginal line from well developed to obsolete;
uns number and size of submarginal ocelli extremely variable, also within the same population;
unf light ring around the ocelli more developed and elongated in f. *striatula*

ssp *biocellata* Staudinger, 1901 **comb. nov.**
Triphysa phryne biocellata Staudinger, 1901, in Staudinger & Rebel Catal. Lep. Pal. Fauna: 67
Type locality: Amdo [Qinghai lake region, China]
ups white marginal line evident;
uns ocelli well developed and often pupillated;
unf ocelli in spaces 2 and 3 well developed, as in *T. phryne*

ssp *gartoki* Bang-Haas, 1929 **comb. nov.**
Triphysa phryne gartoki Bang-Haas, 1929, Horae Macrol. 1: 50
Type locality: Gartok, Thibet occ. [Garyarsa, W. Tibet]
ups white marginal line evident;
uns light suffusion covering almost completely the dark brown ground colour;
unh submarginal ocelli very small

ssp *glacialis* Bang Haas, 1912
Triphysa glacialis Bang Haas, 1912, Deut. ent. Zeit. [Iris] 26: 105
Type locality: Arasagun-Gol [Arshan, E. Sayan]
   – *sacha* Korshunov, 1996, Addenda and Corrigenda to "Butterflies of the Asian part of the Russia": 30
ups white marginal line usually obsolete;
unh submarginal ocelli usually less and smaller than in nominal *dohrnii*

ssp *nervosa* Motschulsky, 1866
Triphysa nervosa Motschulsky, 1866, Bull. Soc. imp. Nat. Moscou 39: 189
Type locality: Japon [mistake: no *Triphysa* species is found in Japan]
   – *albovenosa* Erschoff, 1877, Horae Soc. ent. ross. 12: 336
   – *tscherskii* Grum-Grshimailo, 1899, Annu. Mus. zool. St. Petersbourg 4: 461
   – *yonsaensis* Im Hong An, 1988, Bull. Acad. Sci. P. R. Korea 3: 48
ups white marginal line obsolete;
uns submarginal ocelli absent or very small

TAXONOMIC NOTE
The well known tendency of many Satyrids and particularly of many *Coenonympha* species to have the ocellation influenced by the altitude and/or by climatic differences suggests to attribute to a single species all the very different forms found in the *dohrnii* complex.
Nevertheless the fact that in N. Mongolia and Transbaikalia the range of *glacialis-nervosa* overlaps that of *biocellata* is not easy to explain even in a higly polymorphic species. So an other view is that there are two different species, with the same shape of the male genitalia (anyway sharply different from those of *T. phryne*): *dohrnii*, that includes the subspecies *glacialis* and *nervosa*, and *biocellata* that includes the subspecies *gartoki*

RANGE
ssp *dohrnii*: S. Siberia (Altai and Sayan Mts.)
ssp *biocellata*: N. W. China, Mongolia
ssp *gartoki*: W. Tibet
ssp *glacialis*: Transbaikalia, N. Mongolia, Yakutia
ssp *nervosa*: Amur, N. E. China, N. Korea, N. and N. E. Siberia

SELECTED REFERENCES
Gorbunv (2001)

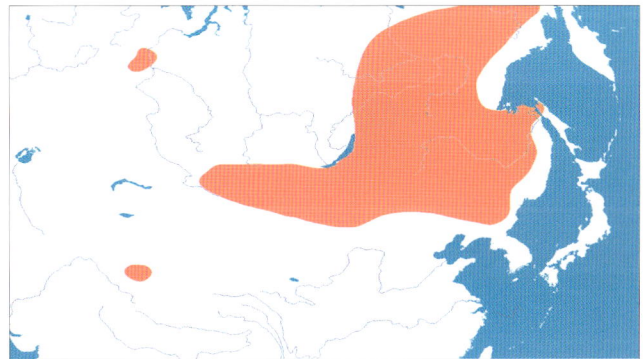

genus **SINONYMPHA** Lee, 1974

Sinonympha Lee, 1974, Acta Ent. Sinica 17: ?
Type species: *Sinonympha amoena* Lee, 1974

DIAGNOSTIC CHARACTERS
antennae short;
palpi long and slender;
forewing base of subcostal and cubital veins swollen;
forewing cell short and broad

RANGE
the only known species is found in Sichuan (China)

CHECKLIST OF THE SPECIES
amoena Lee, 1974

SINONYMPHA AMOENA Lee, 1974

Sinonympha Lee, 1974, Acta Ent. Sinica 17: ?
Type locality: Minshan Mts., Sichuan

DIAGNOSTIC CHARACTERS
ups ground colour whitish with large submarginal ocelli;
uns large submarginal ocelli with prominent pupils

RANGE
Sichuan (China)

♂ ups

♀ ups

♂ uns

Wenchuan, Sichuan, China

♀ uns

road Lixian - Wenchuan,
Sichuan, China

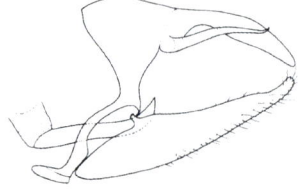

♂ genitalia
from Chou (1998)

Bibliography

A.A.V.V. 1987. *Les papillons de jour et leurs biotopes*. Bale: Ligue Suisse pour la Protection de la Nature

A.A.V.V. 1999. *International Code of Zoological Nomenclature Fourth Edition*. London: The International Trust for Zoological Nomenclature

Abadjiev, S. 1993. *Butterflies of Bulgaria*. Sofia: Veren Publishers

Abadjiev, S. 2000. Types of Balkan butterflies. II. Eastern Large Heath, Coenonympha rhodopensis Elwes, 1900: type locality and lectotype designation. *Atalanta* 31: 461-466

Ackery, P. R. 1988. Hostplants and classification: a review of Nymphalid butterflies. *Biol. Journal Linnean Society* 33: 95-203

Ackery, P. R., de Jong, R. & Vane-Wright, R. 1999. *The Butterflies: Hedyloidea, Hesperioidea and Papilionoidea. In Lepidoptera, Moths and Butterflies. 1. Evolution, Systematics and Biogeography. Handbook of Zoology* 4: 263-300 Berlin: de Gruyter

Alberti, A. and Fritsch, K. 1983. Ueber einige bemerkenswerte Funde von Lepidopteren aus dem Grossen Kaukasus. *Nota lepid.* 6: 192-202

Alphéraky, S. 1881. Lepidopterese du district de Kouldja et des montaignes environnantes. *Horae Soc. ent. ross.* 16: 334-435

Alphéraky, S. 1887. Diagnoses de quelques lepidopteres inedits du Thibet. *In Romanoff, Mem. Lép.* 3: 403-406

Alphéraky, S. 1889. Lepidopteres rapportes du Thibet par le General N. M. Przewalsky de son voyage de 1884-1885. *In Romanoff, Mem. Lep.* 5: 59-89

Alphéraky, S. 1889. Lepidopteres rapportes de la Chine et de la Mongolie par G. N. Potanine. *In Romanoff, Mem. Lép.* 5: 90-123

Alphéraky, S. 1897. Lepidopteres des provinces chinoises Se-Tchouen et Kham recueillis, en 1893, par M-r G. N. Potanine. *In Romanoff, Mem. Lép.* 9: 83-149

Alphéraky, S. 1897. Memoire sur differentes lepidopteres, tant nouveaux que peu connus, de la faune palearctique. *In Romanoff, Mem. Lép.* 9: 185-227

Alphéraky, S. 1897. Lepidopteren aus Kamtschatka gesammelt von O. Herz. *In Romanoff, Mem. Lép.* 9: 301 - 347

Anikin, V. V., Sachov, S. A. & Zolotuhin, V. V. "Fauna lepidopterologica Volgo-Uralensis" 150 years later: changes and additions. Part 1. Rhopalocera. *Atalanta* 24: 89-120

Aoyama, J. 1998. *Butterflies of China*. Tokyo: Tokai University Press

Arheilger, T. 1980. Beschreibung einer Zucht von Melanargia galathea magdalenae R. *Nachr. Ent. Ver. Apollo* 1: 72

Balint, Z. and Olivier, A. 2001. Butterfly species-group taxa from the Balkans and western Anatolia attributed to Imre Frivaldszky (1799-1870). *Ann. Hist.-Nat. Mus. nat. Hung.* 93: 151-198

Bang-Haas, O. 1912. Neue oder wenig bekannte palaearktische Macrolepidopteren. IV. *Deut. ent. Zeit. [Iris]* 26: 103-110

Bang-Haas, O. 1927. *Horae Macrolepidopterologicae regionis palaearcticae Volumen I.* Dresden-Blasewitz

Benyamini, D. 1990. *A Field Guide to the Butterflies of Israel including Butterflies of Mt. Hermon and Sinai*. Keter Publishing House

Benyamini, D. 1993. The butterflies of Mt Hermon. *Linneana Belgica* 14: 167-204

Bianchini, R. 1994. Melanargia galathea Linné, 1758, et ses formes individuelles voisines de tenebrosa dans les Alpes-Maritimes. *Alexanor* 18: 503-504

Boillat, H. 1986. Biologie et statut taxinomique de Coenonympha thyrsis Freyer. Description des etats pre-imaginaux. *Alexanor* 14: 263-278

Boillat, H. 1989. Coenonympha (superspecies dorus) austauti Oberthür. Etude taxinomique et biogeographique. *Alexanor* 15: 393-417

Boillat, H. 1990. Coenonympha (superspecies gardetta) orientalis Rebel Mise au point taxinomique. *Alexanor* 16: 395-412

Bretherton, R. F. 1966. A Distribution List of the Butterflies (Rhopalocera) of Western and Southern Europe. *Trans. Soc. Br. Ent.* 17: 1-94

Bridges, C. A. 1988. *Catalogue of Family-group and Genus-group names (Lepidoptera : Rhopalocera)*. Urbana, Illinois: Charles A. Bridges

Bridges, C. A. 1993. *Bibliography (Lepidoptera : Rhopalocera) (Second edition)*. Urbana, Illinois: Charles A. Bridges

Brower, A. V. Z. 2000. Phylogenetic relationship among the Nymphalidae, inferred from partial sequences of the wingless gene. *Proc. R. Soc. Lond.* B267: 1201-1211

Bryk, F. 1947. Zur Kenntnis der Grossschmetterlinge von Korea. *Ark. Zool.* 38A (3): 1-74

Bustillo, G. M. and Fernandez-Rubio, F. 1974. *Mariposas de la Peninsula Iberica. Rhopaloceros.* Instituto Nacional para la Conservacion de la Naturalez, Madrid

Castro de, E. 1983. Los Rhopalocera ibericos: claves para su determinacion. *SHILAP Revta. lepid.* 44: 323-330

Chou, I. 1994. *Monographia Rhopalocerorum Sinensium*. Henan: Henan Scientific and Thecnological Publishing House

Chou, I. 1998. *Classification and Identification of Chinese Butterflies*. Henan: Henan Scientific and Thecnological Publishing House

Collier, A. E. 1955. A Note on Agapetes (Melanargia) galathea L. ab. aperta Rebel. *Ent. Rec.* 67: 1

Corbet, G. B. 1978. *The Mammals of the Palearctic Region: a taxonomic review*. London and Ithaca: Cornell University Press

Coutsis, J. G. 1972. List of Grecian Butterflies: additional records. 1969-1971 *Ent. Rec.* 84: 145

Coutsis, J. G. 1977. Notes Concerning the Taxonomic Status I. 1998. *Classification and Identification of Chinese Butterflies* . Henan: Henan Scientific and Thecnological Publishing Houseof Coenonympha thyrsis Freyer. *Ent. Rec.* 89: 1-2

D'Abrera, B. 1990. *Butterflies of the Holartic Region. Part I.* Victoria: Hill House

D'Abrera, B. 1992. *Butterflies of the Holartic Region. Part II.* Victoria: Hill House

Davenport, D. 1941. The butterflies of the Satyrid genus Coenonympha. *Bull. Harvard Mus. Comp. Zool.* 87: 215-349

Dennis, R. L. H. 1972. A Biometrical Study of a Welsh Colony of the Large Heath Butterflies, Coenonympha tullia Muller. *Entomologist* 105: 313-326

Descimon, H. and Renon, C. 1975. Melanisme et facteurs climatiques: I – Etude biometrique de la variation de Melanargia galathea (Linné) en France. *Arch. Zool. exp. gen.* 116: 255-292

Draeseke, J. 1925. Die Schmetterlinge der Stotznerschen Ausbeute. *Deut. ent. Zeit. Iris* 39: 48-57

Dubatolov, V. V. 1997. New data on taxonomy of Lycaenidae, Nymphalidae and Satyridae of the Asian part of Russia. *Far Eastern Entomologist* 44: 1-12

Dubatolov, V. V. 2002. Web site of Siberian Zoological Museum. http://szmn.eco.nsc.ru/index.html

Ebert, G., Gross, F. J., Rose, K. and Wagener, S. 1975. Bitraege zur Kenntnis der Rhopaloceren Irans. *J. ent. Soc. Iran* Suppl. 1: 3-47

Eckweiler, W. & Hofmann, P. 1980. Verzeichnis iranischer Tagfalter. *Apollo* Suppl. 1: 1-27

Ehlrich, P. R. 1958. The comparative morphology, phylogeny and higher classification of the butterflies. *Univ. Kansas Sc. Bull.* 39: 305-370

Eitschberger, U. 1971. Eine neue Subspecies von Melanargia ines aus Andalusien. *Ent. Z. Frankfurt.* 81: 145-154

Eitschberger, U. and Steininger, H. 1976. Otra contribution para el estudio de Melanargia ines henrike Eischberger, 1972. *Revista Lepidopt.* 4: 159-162

Elwes, H. J. 1900. On the Butterflies of Bulgaria. *Trans. ent. Soc. Lond.* 1900: 183-206

Elwes, H. J. 1906. On the Lepidoptera collected by the Officers on the recent Tibet Frontier Commission. *Proc. Zool. Soc. Lond.* 33: 479-485

Emmet, A. H. and Heath, J. 1989. *The Moths and Butterflies of Great Britain and Ireland*. Colchester: Harley Books

Ercolino, M. 1997. *Un approccio quantitativo allo studio della variazione geografica delle Melanargia del gruppo larissa. Tesi sperimentale in zoologia.* Università degli studi di Roma "La Sapienza".

Erschoff, N. G. 1874. Lepidoptera. *In Fedtschenko Reise in Turkestan* 2: 1-127

Erschoff, N. G. 1885. Verzeichniss von Schmetterlingen aus Central-Sibirien. *In Romanoff, Mem. Lép.* 2: 208-211

Evans, W. H. 1932a. *The identification of the Indian butterflies*. Second Edition. Madras: Bombay nat. Hist. Soc.

Fernandez-Rubio, F. 1991. *Guia de Mariposas Diurnas de la Peninsula Iberica, Baleares, Canarias, Azores y Madera*. Madrid: Ediciones Piramide

Ford, E. B. 1945. *Butterflies*. London: Collins

Forster, W. 1961. Rhopalocera in Lobbichler, *Lepidoptera der Deutschen Nepal-Expedition 1955*. Veroff. zool. StSamml., Münch.

Forster, W. and Wohlfhart, T.A. 1976. *Die schmetterlinge Mitteleuropas. Band II Tagfalter.* Stuttgart: Franckh'sche Verlagshandlund

Fruhstorfer, H. 1916. Neue Rassen von Melanargia galathea. *Soc. ent.* 31: 33-34

Fruhstorfer, H. 1917. Neue Melanargia galathea-Rassen. *Soc. ent.* 32: 5-6

Gaede, M. 1931. *Lepidopterorum Catalogus Partes 43, 46 et 48. Satyridae*. Berlin: W. Junk

Gaede, M. 1939. In Seitz A. *Les Macrolepidopteres du Globe. I Partie. Les macrolepidopteres de la Region Paleartique. Suppl.* 1: 154-184 Paris: Le Moult

Gomez Bustillo, M. R. and Fernandez-Rubio, F. 1974. *Mariposas de la Peninsula Iberica.* Madrid: Ministerio de Agricultura

Gorbunov, P. Y. 2001. *The Butterflies od Russia: classification, genitalia, keys for identification.* Ekaterinburg: Thesis

Gross, F. J. 1954. Beitrag zur Unterscheidung von Coenonympha arcania L. und gardetta de Prunner. *Z. wien. ent. Ges.* 39: 372-384

Grum-Grshimailo G. E. 1890. Le Pamir et sa faune Lepidopterologique. *In Romanoff, Mem. Lép.* 4: 1-577

Grum-Grshimailo, G. E. 1895. Lepidoptera Palaearctica Nova. *Horae Soc. ent. ross.* 29: 290-293

Hanus, J. 1996. New butterfly taxa from Kirghizia. *Atalanta* 27: 203-210

Harada, M. and Tateishi, T. 1995. A memorandum of early stages in Chinese butterflies. *Butterflies* 10: 22-35

Harvey, D. J. 1991. *Higher classification of the Nymphalidae. Appendix B. In: Nijhout, H. F. (ed.) The Development and Evolution of Butterfly Wing Patterns.* Washington: Smithsonian Inst. Press

Hemming, F. 1933. Hoalrctic butterflies: miscellaneous notes on nomenclature. *Entomologist* 66: 275-279

Hemming, F. 1967. The generic names of the butterflies and their type-species. *Bull. Br. Mus. nat. Hist. (Ent.)* Suppl. 9: 1-509

Henriksen, H. J. & Kreutzer, I. 1982. *The butterflies of Scandinavia in nature.* Odense: Skandinavisk Bogforlag

Hesselbarth, G., Oorschot, van H., Wagener, S. 1995. *Die Tagfalter der Turkei.* Bocholt: Selbstverlag Sigbert Wagener

Higgins, L. G. 1969. An Undescribed European Butterfly. *Entomologist* 102: 60

Higgins, L. G. 1975. *The Classification of European Butterflies.* London: Collins

Higgins, L. G. 1977. New Palaearctic Butterflies. *Ent. Rec.* 89: 189-191

Higgins, L. G. and Riley, N. D. 1970. *A field guide to the butterflies of Britain and Europe.* London: Collins

Houlbert, C. 1922. Contribution a l'etude des Melanargiinae de Chine et de Siberie. *Etud. Lep. Comp.* 19 (2): 117-163

Huang, R. & Murayama, S. 1992. Butterflies of Xinjiang Province, China. *Tyo to Ga* 43: 1-22

Igarashi, Y. 2001. *The Butterflies of Central Mongolia.* Tokyo: Stage

Jaksic, P. N. 1988. *Provisional distribution maps of the butterflies of Yugoslavia.* Zagreb: Societas Entomologica Jugoslavica

Jaksic, P. N. 1998. *Male genitalia of butterflies on Balcan peninsula with a check-list.* Bratislava: Frantisek Slamka

Jutzeler, D. 1994. Okologie und erste Stande des Italienischen Schachbretttes Melanargia arge (Sulzer, 1776). *Nota lepid.* 16: 213-232

Jutzeler, D. 1994. La signification des variantes vertes et brunes des chenilles de Melanargia lachesis (Hübner, 1790). *Linneana Belgica* 14: 335-350

Jutzeler, D., Russo, L. and de Bros, E. 1995. Les premieres etats de Malanargia russiae (Esper, 1787) de Le Murge (Pouille, I) et recherches sur la variabilité de ce taxon. *Linneana Belgica* 15: 182-188

Jutzeler, D. and de Bros, E. 1996. Elevage de Coenonympha corinna corinna (Hübner, 1804) de Sardaigne. Notes sur la repartition de l'espece C. corinna. *Bull. Soc. ent. Mulhouse* 1996: 25-32

Jutzeler, D. Biermann, H. and de Bros, E. 1996. Elevage de Coenonympha corinna elbana (Staudinger, 1901) du Monte Argentario (Toscane, Italie) avec explication geologique de l'aire de repartition du complexe corinna. *Linneana Belgica* 15: 332-347

Jutzeler, D., Grillo, N., Russo, L., Nardelli, U. and de Bros, E. 1996. Position taxinomique et biologie de Malanargia pherusa (Boisduval, 1833) de Sicile selon les stades pre-imaginaux. *Linneana Belgica* 15: 203-213

Jutzeler, D. and de Bros, E. 1997. Ecologie, elevage et statut taxinomique de Coenonympha corinna trettaui (Gross, 1970) de l'Isola di Capraia (Toscane, Italie). *Linneana Belgica* 16: 70-78

Jutzeler, D. 1998. Coenonympha gardetta lecerfi (De Lesse, 1949), une ssp. isolée du complexe gardetta des Monts du Forez (Puy-de-Dome, Auvergne, F.). *Linneana Belgica* 16: 192-195

Kawazoe, A. and Wakabayashi, M. 1976. *Colored illustrations of the butterflies of Japan.* Uemachi: Hoikusha Publishing

Kirby, W. F., 1894. *A Hand-book of the order Lepidoptera.* London

Koçak, A. O. 1976. A new subspecies of Melanargia Larissa from Turkey. *Atalanta* 7: 40-41

Koçak, A. O. 1977. New Lepidoptera from Turkey V. *Atalanta* 8: 126-147

Kocman, S. 1995. Some new subspecies of the genus Parnassius, Boloria and Coenonympha from China. *Lambillionea* 95: 63-67

Kocman, S. 1996. Some new subspecies of the genus Parnassius and Coenonympha from China. *Lambillionea* 96: 37-42

Korb, S. K. 1999. Contribution a la conaissance du genre Coenonympha Hubner, (1819): Cononympha tullia tshonkurtshakus ssp. n. des monts Alexandre (Kirghizistan). *Alexanor* 20: 387-389

Korshunov, Y. P. 1972. Catalogue of diurnal butterflies of the fauna of the U.S.S.R. I. *Ent. Obozr.* 51: 136-154

Korshunov, Y. P. 1972. Catalogue of diurnal butterflies of the fauna of the U.S.S.R. II. *Ent. Obozr.* 51: 352-368

Korshunov, Y. P. 1977. Diurnal butterflies of the Mongolian People's Republic, II [in Russian]. *Nasekomye Mongol.* 5: 649-681

Korshunov, Y. 1996, *Addenda and Corrigenda to "Butterflies of the Asian part of Russia".* Novosibirsk

Korshunov, Y. 1998. *Addenda and Corrigenda to "Butterflies of the Asian part of Russia" (2).* Novosibirsk

Korshunov, Y. P. and Solyanikov, V. P. 1976. Diurnal butterflies of the Mongolian People's Republic [in Russian]. *Nasekomye Mongol.* (4): 403-458

Korshunov, Y. P. and Gorbunov, P. 1995. *Butterflies of the Asian part of Russia* Ekaterinburg: Ural Univ. Press [in Russian]

Krzywicki, M. 1966. *Klucze do oznaczania owadow Polski. Lepidoptera. Satyridae.* Warsaw: Panstwowe Wydawnictwo Naukowe

Kudrna, O. 1985. *Butterflies of Europe Volume 1 Concise Bibliography of European Butterflies.* Wiesbaden: Aula-Verlag

Kudrna, O. 1990. *Butterflies of Europe Volume 2 Introduction to Lepidopterology.* Wiesbaden: Aula-Verlag

Kurentzov, A. I. 1970. *The butterflies of the Far East USSR.* Leningrad: Academy of Sciences of USSR [in Russian]

Lafranchis, T. 2000. *Les papillons de jour de France, Belgique et Luxembourg et leurs chenilles.* Mèze: editions Biotope

Larsen, T. B. 1974. *Butterflies of Lebanon.* Beirut: C.N.R.S.

Larsen, T. B. 1983. Insects of Saudi Arabia. Lepidoptera, Rhopalocera. *Fauna Saudi Arabia* 5: 333-478

Larsen, T. B. 1984. *Butterflies of Saudi Arabia and its neighbours.* London & Riyadh: Stacey International

Larsen, T. B. and Nakamura, I. 1983. The butterflies of East Jordan. *Ent. Gaz.* 34: 135-208

Lee, C. 1992. *Atlas of Chinese butterflies.* [in Chinese]

Lee, S.-M. 1982. *Butterflies of Korea.* Seoul: Editorial Commitee of Insecta Koreana

Leech, J. H. 1892-1894. *Butterflies from China, Japan and Korea.* London: R. H. Porter

Leraut, P. 1990. Contribution a l'etude des Satyrinae de France. *Entomol. Gallica* 2: 8-19

Lesse de, H. 1949. Contribution a l'etude du genre Coenonympha. *Lambillionea* 49: 68-80

Lesse de, H. 1971. Une nouvelle sous espece de Melanargia galathea L. *Alexanor* 7: 156-158

Lhonoré, J. 1998. *Biologie, ecologie et repartition de quatre especes de Lepidopteres Rhopaloceres dans l'Ouest de la France.* Rapport d'etudes de l'OPIE, Vol. 2 decembre 1998

Lukhtanov, V.A.and Lukhtanov, A.G. 1994. *Die Tagfalter Nordwestasiens.* Herausgeber: Dr. Ulf Eitschberger, Marktleuthen

Manley, W. B. L. and Allcard, H. G. 1970. *A field guide to the butterflies and burnets of Spain.* Hampton: Classey

Martin, J. A. and Pashley, D. P. 1992. Molecular systematic analysis of butterfly family ans some subfamily relationships. *Ann. ent. Soc. Amer.* 82: 127-139

Martin, J. A., Gilles, A. and Descimon, H. 2000. Molecular Phylogeny and Evolutionary Patterns of the European Satyrids as Revealed by Mitochondrial Gene Sequences. *Molecular Phylogenetics and Evolution* 15: 70-82

Mazel, R. 1986. Contacts parapatriques entre Melanargia galathea L. et M. lachesis Hübner. *Nota Lepid.* 9: 81-91

Merceron, E. 1998. Notes coleopterologiques et lepidopterologiques. *Bull. Soc. en. Mulhouse* 1998: 14-15

Mensi, P., Lattes, A., Cassulo, L., Cinti, R. and Balletto, E. 1990. Electrophoretic studies in the genus Melanargia Meigen, 1828. *J. Res. Lepid.* 29: 11-20

Merit, X. C. 1996. Les formes claires de Melanargia galathea (Linné, 1758) en Ardèche septentrionale: bilan et proportion. *Linneana Belgica* 15: 219-224

Miller, L. D. 1968. The higher classification, phylogeny and zoogeography of the Satyridae. *Mem. amer. ent. Soc.* 24: 1-174

Montero, A. and Pierce, N. E. 2001. Phylogeny of Byciclus inferred from COI, COII and Ef-la gene sequences. *Mol. Phylogenet. Evol.* 18: 264-281

Mori, T. & Cho, F. 1938. A list of Butterflies in Machoukuo with Descriptions of two new Species. *Rep. Inst. scient. Res., Machoukuo* 2: 1-102

Murayama, S. 1986. Remarks and corrections of Rhopalocera from Far East Asia with description of two new species and four new subspecies. *Entomotaxonomia* 8: 59-62

Murayama, S. 1987. Some new butterflies from Far East Asia. *The Nature & Insects* 22: 41-43

Nardelli, U. and Benedetto, G. 1994. Melanargia pherusa Boisduval 1833: Biologie, Okologie, Morphologie und Verbreitung im Vergleich mit Melanargia arge Sulzer 1776. *Nachr. Ent. Ver. Apollo* 15: 87-108

Nardelli, U., Olivares, J. et al. 1998 *Linneana Belgica* 16: 183-191

Nekrutenko, Y. P. 1985. *Butterflies of Krimea.* Kiev: Namkova Dumka

Nekrutenko, Y. P. 1990. *The Butterflies of the Caucasus.* Kiev

Nice, C. C. and Shapiro, A. M. 2001. Patterns of morphological, biochemical and molecular evolution in Oeneis chryxus complex: a test of historical biogeographical hypotesis. *Mol. Phylogenet. Evol.* 20: 111-123

Niceville, L. de 1882. *The Butterflies of India, Burma and Ceylon.* Calcutta: Calcutta Central Press Co.

Nordstrom, F. 1935. Schwedisch-chinesische wissenschaftliche Expedition nach den nordwestlichen Provinzen Chinas. *Ark. Zool.* 27A: 1-37

Oberthür, C. 1876. Etude sur la Faune des Lepidopteres de l'Algerie. *Etud. ent.* 1: 9-74

Oberthür, C. 1881. Lepidopteres d'Algérie. *Etud. ent.* 6: 41-96

Oberthür, C. 1891. Nouveaux Lepidopteres d'Asie. *Etud. ent.* 15: 9-25

Oberthür, C. 1894. Lepidopteres d'Europe, d'Algerie, d'Asie & d'Oceanie. *Etud. ent.* 19: x + 41 pp

Oberthür, C. 1909. Notes pour servir a etablir la Faune Francaise et Algerienne des Lepidopteres. *Etudes de Lepidopterologie Comparee* 3: 101-404

Oberthür, C. 1910. Notes pour servir a etablir la Faune Francaise et Algerienne des Lepidopteres (Suite). *Etudes de Lepidopterologie Comparée* 4: 15-664

Oberthür, C. 1911. Supplement aux Notes pour servir a etablir la Faune Francaise et Algerienne des Lepidopteres. *Etudes de Lepidopterologie Comparée* 5: 183-225

Oberthür, C. 1912. Plate 123 *Etudes de Lepidopterologie Comparée* 6: Pl. 123

Oberthür, C. 1922. *Les Lepidopteres du Maroc.* Etud. Lep. comp. 19: 13-402

Pamperis, L. N. 1997. *The Butterflies of Greece.* Larissa: Bastas-Plessas

Park, K. T. and Kim, S. S. 1997. *Insects of Korea Series 1. Atlas of Butterflies.* Korea: Korea Research Institute for Bioscience and Biotechnology

Porter, A. H., Schneider, R. W. and Price, B. A. 1995. Wing pattern and allozyme relationships in the Coenonympha arcania group, emphasising the C. gardetta - darwiniana contact area at Bellwald, Switzerland. *Nota lepid.* 17: 155-174

Reichl, E. R. 1975. Die Rassenbildung von Melanargia galathea L. im westlichen Friaul. *Zeit. ArbGem. ost. Ent.* 26: 33-40

Rojo, J. C. S. 1997. Una nueva subespecie iberica de Coenonympha dorus (Esper, 1782). *Boletin de la SEA* 18: 66-67

Romanoff, N. M. G. 1884. Les Lepidopteres de la Transcaucasie. *In Romanoff, Mem. Lép.* 1: 1-92

Rothschild, W. 1917. Supplemental notes to Mr. Charles Oberthur's Faune des Lepidopteres de la Barbarie, with lists of the specimens contained in the Tring Museum. *Novit. zool.* 61-120

Rowland-Brown, H. 1913. The distribution and variation of Coenonympha tiphon in the United Kingdom. *Etudes de Lepidopterologie Comparee* 7: 85-193

Russo, L. 1996. Considerations sur la validité des sous-espèces géographiques de Melanargia arge (Sulzer, 1776). *Linneana Belgica* 15: 229-252

Sakai, S. 1981. *Butterflies of Afghanistan.* Tokyo: Kodansha [In Japanese]

Sbordoni, V., Fani, C., Cesaroni, M. and Lucarelli, M. 2002. Molecular phylogeny and biogeography of the Satyrid genus Callerebia an allied taxa: an attempt to trace the origin of the Himalayan faunal elements. *4th International Conference on the Biology of Butterflies, Leiden 2002, The Netherlands,* Abstracts: 27

Schaider, P. and Jaksic, P. 1989. *Die Tagfalter von jugoslawisch Mazedonien.* Ljubljana: Janez Plesko

Scott, J. A. 1986. *The Butterflies of North America.* Standford, California: Standford University Press

Seitz, A. *Les Macrolepidopteres du Globe. Les Macrolepidopteres de la Region Paleartique. 1er Volume. Diurnes Paleartiques.* Paris: Le Moult

Seitz, A. *Les Macrolepidopteres du Globe. Les Macrolepidopteres de la Region Paleartique. Tome I. Diurnes Paleartiques. Supplement.* Paris: Le Moult

Seok, D. M. 1939. *A synonymic list of butterflies of Korea (Tyosen).* Seoul: Royal Asiatic Society

Settele, J., Feldmann, R. and Reinhardt, R. 2000. *Die Tagfalter Deutschlands.* Stuttgart: Ulmer

Shirozu, T. 1960. *Butterflies of Formosa in colour.* Osaka Hoikusha

Smith, C. 1993. *Illustrated checklist of Nepal's butterflies.* Lashkar: Rohit Kumar

Standfuss, M. 1892. *Lepidopterologisches. In Romanoff, Mem. Lép.* 6: 659-669

Staudinger, O. 1886. Centralasiatische Lepidopteren. *Stett. ent. Z.* 47: 193-215

Staudinger, O. 1887. Neue arten und Varietaten von Lepidopteren aus dem Amur-gebiet. *In Romanoff, Mem. Lép.* 3: 126-232

Staudinger, O. 1892. Die Macrolepidopteren des Amurgebiets. *In Romanoff, Mem. Lép.* 6: 83-658

Staudinger, O. and Rebel, H. 1901. *Catalog der Lepidopteren des Palearctischen Faunegebiets.* Berlin: R. Friedlander and Sohn

Takahashi, M., Tetsuka, Y. & Ichikawa, T. 1997. Butterflies from Sakhalin, Far Eastern Russia, 1995-96. *Butterflies* 18: 4 - 22

Talbot, G. 1947. *The Fauna of British India, including Ceylon and Burma. Butterflies Vol. II.* London: Taylor and Francis Ltd

Tarrier, M. 1995. Nouveaux taxa des Atlas marocaine. *Alexanor* 19: 195-213

Tatarinov, A. and Dolgin, M. 1999. *Fauna of the North-East of the European Russia. Butterflies* [in Russian]. S. Petersburg: Nauka

Tennent, J. 1996. *The Butterflies of Morocco, Algeria and Tunisia.* Wallingford: Gem Publishing Company

Thomson, G. 1980. *The Butterflies of Scotland A Natural History.* London: Croom Helm

Tolman, T. 1997. *Butterflies of Britain and Europe.* London: HarperCollins

Torres, E., Lees, D. C., Vane-Wright, R. I. Kremen, C. Leonard. J. A. and Wayne, R. K. 2001. Examining monophyly in a large radiation of Madagascan butterflies based on mitochondrial DNA data. *Mol. Phylogenet. Evol.* 20: 460-473

Tshikolovets, V. V. 1995. *A catalogue of the Type-specimens of the Lepidoptera in the Scmalhausen Institute of Zoology, National Academy of Sciences of Ukraine, Kiev.* Ed. Y. P. Nekrutenko

Tshikolovets, V. V. 1997. *The butterflies of Pamir.* Bratislava: František Slamka

Tshikolovets, V. V. 1998. *The butterflies of Turkmenistan.* Kyiv- Brno

Tshikolovets, V. V. 2000. *The butterflies of Uzbekistan.* Kyiv- Brno

Tshikolovets, V. V. 2002. *The Butterflies of Transbaikal Siberia.* Brno - Kyiv: Vadim V. Tshikolovets

Turati, E. 1921. Lepidotteri di Cirenaica raccolti dal Prof. A. Ghigi durante l'escursione organizzata dal Touring Club Italiano nel mese d'aprile 1920. *Atti Soc. ital. Sc. nat.* 60: 211-229

Turati, E. 1934. Novità di Lepidotterologia in Cirenaica. *Atti Soc. ital. Sc. nat.* 73: 159-212

Tuzov, V. K., Bogdanov, P. V., Devyatkin, A. L., Kaabak, L. V., Korolev, V. A., Murzin, V. S., Samodurov, G. D. and Tarasov, E. A. 1997. *Guide to the Butterflies of Russia and adjacent territories (Lepidoptera, Rhopalocera). Vol. 1.* Sofia-Moscow: Pensoft

Verity, R. 1926. The geographical and seasonal variations of Coenonympha pamphilus L. *Z. wiss. InsektBiol.* 21: 191-208

Verity, R. 1953. *Le farfalle diurnde d'Italia Volume Quinto Divisione Papilionida Sezione Nymphalina Famiglia Satyridae.* Florence: Casa Editrice Marzocco

Wagener, S. 1959–1961. *Monographie der ostasiatischen Formen der Gattung Melanargia Meigen.* Stuttgart: E. Schweizerbart'sche

Wagener, S. 1975. Der vorderasiatischen Formen der Melanargia russiae (Esper, 1784). *J. ent. Soc. Iran* 1(suppl.): 47-62

Wagener, S. 1976. Beitrage zur Kenntnis der Rhopaloceren Irans. *J. ent. Soc. Iran* 3: 75-80

Wagener, S. 1980a. Beitrage zur Kenntnis der Rhopaloceren Irans 12. Die vorderasiatischen Formen der Melanargia russiae (Esper, 1784). *Atalanta* 11: 29-39

Wagener, S. 1980b. Beitrage zur Kenntnis der Rhopaloceren Irans 13. Bemerkungen zu Melanargia evartiane Wagener, 1976. *Atalanta* 11: 39-42

Wagener, S. 1983a. Zur Taxonomie, Nomenklatur und Verbreitung von Melanargia titea (Klug, 1832). *Nota Lepid.* 6: 175-188

Wagener, S. 1983b. Zwei neue Melanargia-Formen aus Anatolien. *Atalanta* 14: 247-299

Wagener. 1984a. Struktur und Skulptur der Eihüllen einiger Melanargia-Arten. *Andrias* 3: 73-96

Wagener. 1984b. Melanargia lachesis est-elle une espece differente de Melanargia galathea Linnaeus 1758, oui ou non? *Nota Lepid.* 7: 375-386

Wakeham-Dawson, A. 1997. A comparison of specimens of Melanargia russiae (Esper, 1784) from Greece and Spain. *Ent. Gaz.* 48: 225-229

Warren, B. C. S. 1930. A definition of the Satyrid Genera: Erebia, Callerebia, Paralasa and Erebomorpha. *Ent. Rec.* 42: 103-107

Weiss, J. C. 1979. Description de trios nouvelles sous-especes de Rhopaloceres du Rif Marocain. *Entomops* 48: 271-274

Wiemers, M. 1994. *Differenzierungsmuster bei Artbildungsprozessen: Morphologisch-biometrische und enzymelektrophoretische Untresuchungen am Coenonympha arcania (Linnaeus, 1761) Suprspezies-Komplex.* Bonn: Universitat Bonn Fachbereich Biologie

Wiemers, M. 1998. Coenonympha darwiniana - a hybrid taxon? New insights through allozyme electrophoresis. *Mem. Soc. r. belge Ent.* 38: 41-70

Wiltshire, E. P. 1957. *The Lepidoptera of Iraq.* London: Nicholas Kaye Ltd

Yazaki, Y. 2002. *Butterflies of Mongolia Volume 3 Satyridae.* Kitami: K. Yazaki

Zhiceng, W. 1999. *Monographia of original colred&size Butterflies of China's Northeast.* Jilin: Jilin Scientific and Technological Publishing House

Systematic Index

Principal entries are given in bold type